Hanif Kureishi was born in 1954 and brought up in Bromley, Kent. He read philosophy at King's College, London, where he started to write plays. In 1981 he won the George Devine Award for *Outskirts*, and in 1982 was appointed Writer in Residence at the Royal Court Theatre. In 1984 he wrote the screenplay for *My Beautiful Laundrette*, which subsequently received an Oscar nomination for Best Screenplay. His second film, also directed by Stephen Frears, was *Sammy and Rosie Get Laid*. His novel, *The Buddha of Suburbia*, won the Whitbread Prize for best first novel in 1991. His first feature as a director, *London Kills Me*, was released in 1991. He is currently working on a new novel.

D0727836

Outskirts and Other Plays

THE KING AND ME
OUTSKIRTS
BORDERLINE
BIRDS OF PASSAGE

Hanif Kureishi

faber and faber
LONDON · BOSTON

This collection first published in 1992
by Faber and Faber Limited
3 Queen Square London WC1N 3AU

The King and Me and *Outskirts* were first published in the same volume in 1983 by
John Calder (Publishers) Ltd, London
Borderline was first published by Methuen London Ltd in 1981 in association with
the Royal Court Theatre
Birds of Passage was first published in 1983 by Amber Lane Press Ltd

Photoset by Parker Typesetting Service Leicester
Printed in England by Clays Ltd St Ives plc

This collection © Hanif Kureishi, 1992
Introduction © Hanif Kureishi, 1992

Hanif Kureishi is hereby identified as author of this work in accordance with
Section 77 of the Copyright, Designs and Patents Act 1988

A CIP record for this book is available from the British Library

ISBN 0-571-16307-6

Contents

Introduction

When I was eighteen I wrote a short play, and sent it to the Royal Court Theatre in Sloane Square, London. To me, the Royal Court was hallowed ground, and the walls of its perfect auditorium breathed accomplishment and integrity. The Court believed in itself and never compromised; it was not only the centre of new British writing but was notorious during the 1960s for its political rucks with the theatre censor, the Lord Chamberlain.

Soon I received a reply inviting me to go and see them. Weeks later my father discovered this letter in my bedroom – I'd been too intimidated to reply to it – and persuaded me to go and meet the literary manager, Donald Howarth.

After he'd made some remarks about my play, I expected to be dismissed by Howarth and returned to my dismal life. I dreaded this, but at least something I'd written had been taken seriously. However, Howarth led me into the auditorium and invited me to sit at the back and watch the proceedings. That afternoon Samuel Beckett was standing on stage rehearsing *Footfalls* with Billie Whitelaw. Howarth left me there. I returned several times, and sometimes sat with Beckett in the pub next to the Court. Once he gave me £50 when I needed money for a course I wanted to do.

As a way of participating in the place, I was given a job selling ice-creams and programmes. Howarth also handed me piles of unsolicited manuscripts to write reports on, though I was soon reprimanded for being pitiless. 'You're not writing reviews for the *Evening Standard*,' I was told. There was a Sunday-night production of my short play – productions 'without decor' these were called – and it was the first time I heard actors speak lines I'd written.

I worked at the Court in this way, while attending University during the day, for two years. Nobody voluntarily taught me anything – they were too busy and self-absorbed – but I did my best to learn what I could from the writers, directors and actors working there, who included Peter Gill, Bill Gaskell, Max

Stafford-Clark, Caryl Churchill and Mustapha Matare. I was too earnest, inquisitive and ambitious to be ashamed of collaring busy people and questioning them. Anyway, there were so many factions and quarrels that people were keen to talk, especially about each other.

The obsession of the many professional gossips at the Court, their focus, as it were, was not only sex but class, the origins of those working there and what these meant precisely. When anyone new joined, their sexual proclivity would be established, followed by their class background, what school they had attended and what their parents earned. This dissection had originally been a Marxist tool, a way of clarifying what was fatuous and cruel about England, but it had become self-hatred, a form of categorization, exclusion and contempt. I've never known any group of people more gripped by the aristocracy and the business of the royal family.

It was an excellent education in the arts and in living. The people at the Court were also passionately concerned with plays, with writing, design, acting, directing. I was impressed that they had succeeded in constructing their whole lives around art. Culture mattered to them, it wasn't merely distraction or 'entertainment'; it spoke about life and challenged it. They disputed ferociously about subjects that no one else gave a damn about.

I'd imagined that workers in such a close profession would feel some solidarity with colleagues in other theatres. But the Royal Court famously had a sort of siege mentality, as if talent, truth and especially political comprehension resided here and in few other places. They hated anyone, however accepted by the public, who worked elsewhere, especially if they were vulgar – crowd-pleasing, meretricious, 'theatrical', politically naïve – or even just critically successful. Once I informed a director that I liked a particular play by Tom Stoppard. Soon my remark was being relayed around the building, accompanied by sneers, hilarity and camp jibes. It was weeks before it was forgotten.

When my father bought a book, new or second-hand, he would take a plastic carrier-bag from under the kitchen sink and, using scissors and sticky tape, fashion a plastic cover for the book, to preserve it. This was a function of his love for literature: you cared for books, they weren't disposable. (He'd hate it if anyone asked to borrow one.) But it was a little queer that his library consisted of shiny plastic-covered books with the regalia of 'Marks & Spencer' or 'Russell & Bromley' crossing the spine and cover.

My father's book-love supported a view of the world. He respected people who could speak or write 'good English'. (I noticed this form of respect was common among Indians of a certain age and class.) 'He writes beautiful English,' he'd say of someone, as if this facility were yoked to humane values, and the mellifluous manipulation of sentences would produce people who were good, magnanimous and polite. Early on, I may have unconsciously absorbed this assumption, which might account for my being disconcerted by the behaviour and language of highly educated theatre people when they revealed such spite and biliousness towards each other over something as edifying as a play.

My father owned many collections of short stories, some in translation. I preferred the French and Russian stories, though he had plenty of Saki, Maugham, O'Hendry, Fitzgerald and Hemingway. I soon learned that if I wanted literary happiness, to escape into guaranteed bliss, I could read a story. If the story worked I would be engrossed, simultaneously relishing the moment and straining to reach the end. Afterwards I'd be satisfied, though an especially cunning story would leave me thoughtful: I'd been made to look at something difficult but true about life, something elusive, that perhaps I'd felt but not tangibly recognized until that moment. So I saw that good writing could evoke the unsaid, indicating the mysterious and enigmatic. Language could point to where language could not go.

At this time, the early 1970s, psychology and sociology, the modish student disciplines, were striving to explain human behaviour, usually with a crude and artificial vocabulary, reducing what people actually did to scientific laws, like the physical world. And yet however precise these 'sciences' appeared, the spirit of life evaded their rule-making. Fortunately life has always had its own method, which is art or poetry, the only science capable of delivering to us the meaning of a particular look in someone's eyes.

As I craved these effects (as I still do) I became aware of the separate sources of satisfaction in reading a story. There was the story itself and what it said; and there was the author's craft and skill, the impressive fact that he or she had accomplished this shaping at all. My admiration of sportsmen and musicians, from Miles Davis to Gary Sobers and Jimi Hendrix, shifted to writers; but there was one thing working here: the delight of witnessing an art supremely displayed, and the spectacle of overcoming self, embodied creatively.

I envied anyone who could do these things. I wanted to do them. Succeed or fail, I began to consider art the most worthwhile thing anyone could attempt to do. More than anything I wanted to do it myself.

One day at school, when I was fourteen, I made up my mind to be a writer. It was the first major decision I'd made, the first time I was aware of having a whole life and not just a succession of days. To my surprise, this decision affected everything. I seemed suddenly to have gained direction, volition; the various annoyances of the present were less weighty when there was a future pulling me on. I could detach myself from the life around me because I had a plan of escape. At the same time the present did matter, for the future would be built out of the present. There was both urgency and relief.

I started to dream on paper, amazed at the power of this new magic to transform any daily event into paragraphs, so that little of life need be lost or wasted if words could secure it, control it, reconstitute it.

In 'Why I Write', Orwell notes 'a sort of private world in which I could get my own back for my failure in everyday life', acknowledging that to write is to claim primacy for one's version of experience, and even a form of revenge. But just as no diary is written to be unread, a piece of prose can't merely be a private arrangement of events, but is always an attempt to make contact; otherwise it wouldn't matter what was said or how it was put.

Inevitably I became aware of my clumsiness, of being unable to make words sing, and the difficulty of placing them in apt combinations. I could see it was impossible to know whether or not I was creating that longed-for effect on the reader – I was the only reader. I read repeatedly what I'd written but was unable to distinguish any possible effect. I tried reading my work as if I were someone else, but this, I discerned, was as impossible as seeing the back of your head by leaping in the air and twisting clockwise.

I had to learn about this profession of words, learn the discipline to get started every morning; the patience to repeatedly return to what I'd written, slinging out the best stuff and beginning again, just when I fancied I was getting somewhere; I had to learn to wait for ideas that wouldn't be persuaded. And crucially, I had to extend a talent for isolation, for sitting in a room with the door closed for hours on end, daily. These were the basic requirements for the job.

Using these requirements I hoped my voice would emerge, but this is the hardest thing of all. Your voice is intimately joined with discovering what you feel and think, in other words, with who you are. The difficulty of developing this explains why it is so tempting to put on your best voice for writing. I've seen this often with young writers whose work fails to resemble what is most interesting about them – their self – as if they'd dressed up for a special occasion and were afraid of creasing their trousers.

While this work continued it was being undercut by my uncertainty, by the terror that I was making a mistake in choosing this work at all, that my hopes and ambitions were vain indulgence.

Later, when one thinks of oneself as a writer, partly because what one writes is published, produced and, most importantly, paid for, it's an effort to remember how hard it is to start writing and how much harder it is to keep going. It isn't necessary to the rest of the world that one is a writer, it's merely a high hurdle that one has decided to fling oneself over. So there has to be some bloody-minded, unrelenting determination to continue. From somewhere within, one has to muster more confidence than self-doubt. There has to be obsessiveness too, so that the meaning of one's life is bound up with the arrangement of words and telling of stories. Finally, there has to be love for what one does.

I adored the stories I read, but as I started to write I couldn't help feeling that this tiny skill, this intricate work, rather resembled lace-making. It was elegantly useless, the creation of a *frisson* for a literary minority who were like train-spotters in their numbers and probably in their eccentricity too. This was, after all, the early 1970s, when there was much 'Death of the Novel' talk: not an interesting subject.

But I was aware of one significant thing: of the potency and influence of another language which spoke to millions – pop music. If I read a novel, there was no one to discuss it with, whereas if a hot album came out one felt excluded if one hadn't heard it. The release of a major album was something to get excited about: we couldn't wait to discover what Dylan, the Stones and the Beatles, Bowie and numerous others were thinking. (I believe that the publication of a new novel by Marquez has something like this effect in South America.) Pop music and youth culture were enfolded with a world-wide common vocabulary and code, as incomprehensible to outsiders, it was said, as a discussion between medieval historians. Except that pop music was ever-increasing in its impact. 'The retreat from the word', this was called by George Steiner, as professors marked their papers in university buildings rattling with rock music. It seemed the White Elitist Word had had it.

It is well known that at different times, in different cities, certain arts are primary or central, and at this time it was pop, with London being as important as anywhere in the USA. Britain's cornucopia of music prevented the country from becoming a third-rate cultural outpost, the complete victim of US cultural power. Britain couldn't be entirely Americanized while it continued to generate its own identity through music and fashion and the political culture and activism of its youth. If it wasn't for British pop we'd have had to look to the US for practically all of our contemporary culture – movies, clothes, painting and the novel.

But privacy, the necessary condition for reading and writing, rendered one adrift from the time. There was something furtive or unnatural about writing, compared to the direct emotional exposure, the bodily presence, the palpable force on mind and body, that pop breathed. We listened to music with others, around a record player: and we listened to the radio and watched TV at the same time as millions of others. It looked as if Steiner was right when he said: 'Everywhere a sound-culture seems to be driving back the old authority and verbal order.' Except that it didn't appear regrettable, only inevitable, and anyhow, because the music was so abundant and so good, little was being lost and much gained. But because of this, writing required justification. Being in a rock 'n' roll band didn't. Everyone wanted to be in a band.

Yet it seemed ridiculous to talk about the demise of the need to tell and be told stories. It is this basic love of stories that accounts for people's fascination with soap operas; they may be badly written, acted and directed, but they comfort and compel an enormous audience, night after night. Surely TV alone doesn't have to absorb and satisfy one's appetite for 'Once upon a time . . .'?

Television serials are often shallow; music banal. The appetite for sustained and serious stories, that make demands on the engaged imagination of the reader, that involve the reader's intelligent participation, cannot be fulfilled by television or music. There is a different effort involved, which has clearly not diminished. And there is something necessarily human, both prurient and objective, in our desire to become familiar through complex stories with the lives of others, measuring them against our own in a myriad of ways. Some philosophers in the post-war period have written as if the telling of stories and the ordering they involve is an arbitrary construct slammed on the formless and unpredictable openness of life as it is lived. Yet formlessness, fragmentation and breakdown can only make sense in the context of assumed ordering, connecting and meaning. It would be difficult to say what sort of life or society there could be without stories.

In the 1970s the film industry seemed impossible to break into, and there were few films made in Britain. At the same time, American films – *The Godfather* Parts I and II, *Mean Streets*, *Taxi Driver*, *Jaws*, *Annie Hall*, *The Deer Hunter*, *American Graffiti* –

overwhelmed us. We could make rock 'n' roll – there was nerve and confidence enough for that – but we couldn't touch this. For a start, recent British experience hadn't been as raw or shattering.

And anyway, to me, film didn't seem to be a writer's form; or at least the writers weren't given much weight. No one even knew the names of the writers behind the most famous films, or even those who wrote the films they liked best. It was as if people imagined that the actors made up dialogue, character, story and plot as they went along, and the 'auteur' didn't require a clear map to follow as he 'discovered' his film.

The novel was posh, written by gentlemen like Graham Greene, and published by upper-crust Bloomsbury types. Besides, novel-writing was too solitary for a young man.

But the theatre was lively and often aspired to the condition of pop music, to my mind a great advantage. A festival of 'happenings' and new plays by performance-oriented groups was called 'Come Together' after a Beatles song. And dozens of young people were working in this 'alternative' or 'fringe' theatre. The plays, when they were about anything, concerned left and anarchist politics, sex roles, rebellion and oppression. They flourished all over London, in basements, above pubs, in tents, in the street and even in theatres. They used nudity, insult, music, audience participation and comedy. They attacked the Labour Party from the left. This was good enough for me.

I was among people who felt that what they were doing was not useless: this wasn't lace-making. Political belief gave us ardour.

After the age had caught up with Gramsci's Leninist analysis of hegemony, the whole cultural area was now being seen as political, as presenting values, assumptions, practices, all seemingly invisible, but which kept late capitalism intact. Part of the state's use of force was the coercive nature of implicit ideas, which were, partly, disseminated by the state's media. Naturally, as the media multiplied, its influence was grasped as being politically significant in many ways, as was, therefore, the analysis of its workings and cultural defiance of its paradigms.

The subsidized theatre was relatively free from state, economic or institutional censorship, compared to television and film; it could be an independent political forum, dealing with sexuality, the security services, Northern Ireland and the corruption of politicians and the state, without the obstruction that TV projects sometimes faced. The problem was that the theatre still reached only a small proportion of the population.

Little was gained in numbers or poetry by trying to annex drama to the cathartic ecstasy of a pop concert. The pop audience didn't much like the theatre and if there was rock 'n' roll in a play they found the acting interrupted it. And if anything, this kind of play – using agit-prop, song, caricature and, usually, clenched-fist salutes at the end, in a kind of music-hall on speed – was even more élitist and esoteric than conventional theatre. It rarely appealed to those elusive 'wider audiences', and least of all to the working class it was often about, though not addressed to. It was depressing: there was no breakthrough. Like other vestiges of the 1960s, the fringe became self-indulgent.

The more structured and better-written radical drama of the 1970s –, the plays of Barker, Brenton and Bond, for example – resembled a debate between friends. For a time this was a pleasure; the basic terms were understood. But this also prevented these plays from establishing a hold on the imagination of the public that subsidized them. Once the possibility and therefore the necessity of reaching an unconvinced audience was gone, many writers lost their sense of the aesthetic, as if the theatre were a matter of the amount of morality behind it: they felt their work was worthwhile if the message was commendable. You could sit through some terrible evening and hear the writer or director say in the pub afterwards, 'At least the point was worth making,' confirming a leftish audience in its prejudices just as much as a bourgeois audience was confirmed in its own.

Interestingly, in the 1980s, effective radical drama did emerge on television, where the constraints of being direct, popular, demanding and serious generated *The Boys from the Blackstuff* and *Edge of Darkness*.

Once I'd got started as a writer, at the Royal Court, Riverside Studios and other new writing venues, I never felt alone, never felt I was working in a vacuum, without support. In the politically conscious 1970s there was, in TV and theatre, a liberal desire to encourage work from unmapped and emergent areas. It was a feeling that what was happening in Britain – despite our regret that it wasn't America – was at least more interesting than most of its representations would have you believe, that more vibrant and searching work would come from the telling of new stories, and so editors and literary managers were appointed to seek out new writers.

They required stories about the new British communities, by cultural translators, as it were, to interpret one side to the other. Anyone with one eye open could see that Britain had changed. It wasn't merely a matter of black workers doing the dirty jobs in the hospitals and on the buses. This was the end of something – the psychological loosening of the idea of Empire – and the start of something else, which involved violence, the contamination of racism and years of crisis. The questions that a multi-cultural society had to ask had hardly been put.

If you couldn't write much but wanted to badly enough, the theatres could put you with people who could help. It mattered to the dramaturgs, editors and directors that new writers were developed, that a new culture – not nostalgia, not analysis, not mere entertainment, but a living response – was cultivated.

Just as most musicians, painters or film directors serve some sort of apprenticeship, there is a need for writing-teachers, otherwise only the most confident and resourceful will survive and unnurtured talent will go missing. Numerous different types of writing courses have been established, mainly in America. But this demand has forced an uneven and spurious outcome. There are, for instance, peripatetic, charismatic instructors peddling 'Aristotelian' theories, plot-points and the charm of *Casablanca*, as if formulas extracted from successful works can somehow provide a writer with the imagination to tell his own stories. This hawking of a non-existent secret, trying to freeze something that can only be spontaneous, and impose from without that which can only be born within, appeals to people who prefer the idea of being a writer – and making money (ha!) – to actually putting words on paper. It's rather like teaching tennis by showing tapes of past Wimbledon finals. It is misleading too. These logorrhoeaic sages usually fail to inform their acolytes of the discipline, concentration, sacrifice and determination required to begin making a work of art, because they know it will be discouraging.

There are other courses which at least take place over a useful period, a year say, so that some development can be achieved. But these courses, often clinging to some notion of being 'academic', are often over-intellectual, encouraging students to theorize and conceptualize about their work, with the latest ideas as a starting point, rather than something smelt, seen or felt.

More disturbingly, I have observed and taught writing courses where some of the students prefer to discuss how they will market their work, get an agent at ICM and handle their publicity. Yet they can barely write a postcard, let alone begin their own *Tom Sawyer*. If one were discussing painting, one would talk about the importance of learning to draw from life. The literary equivalent is the ability to write coherent sentences that follow on from one another. Without this, the imagination may fly, but it will never receive form.

So instead of turning out writers, with each university town as crammed with classy scribblers as Paris in the 1860s, we have more and more writing-teachers, courses, word-processors and students trapped in a self-perpetuating system of self-delusion, dishonesty and indifferent education, with teachers who respect every individual's 'creativity', confusing self-expression – legitimate as it is – with the forging of something that is of interest to others. It is often a racket, the teaching-writing game, mainly for the benefit of the teachers. Many real writers have subsidized their work by this kind of employment; it's hardly surprising that they haven't blown the whistle on it. And bad writers can glean status and respect from a position that keeps them from their desk.

The best teachers know that every piece of writing, if it is alive, sets its own terms and has its own voice and taste. It is this which has to be creatively released. So the talent essential to a teacher, the basis of an intimate and helpful response, is the ability to read – to feel and grasp what the possibilities of the piece are, gauging not only the achievement but what the writer is attempting, what has not quite been reached. This literary clairvoyance is a rare and important skill. (It is one usually lacking – or not valued – in the film industry, where it is required the most.)

In 1981, when I was working in a bookshop, Max Stafford-Clark, artistic director of the Royal Court, asked me to write a play for, or rather with, Joint Stock. I was thrilled: Joint Stock was one of the best British touring companies, and had developed a unique way of making plays. After casting, the actors, writer and director would spend six months researching the idea, improvising around characters met and gathering information about the subject, whether it be the world of horse-racing, the financial markets, life in a Chinese village, or our particular pitch, the lives of immigrants and their children in Southall, a predominantly Sikh area of West London. After this period of collective effort, the writer would spend ten weeks writing the script, using the gathered material. Eventually the play would be rehearsed in the normal way, though over a longer period than is usual in the British theatre, allowing more valuable time for rewriting.

The idea of working like this was to produce well-informed drama about contemporary events, a mixture of information about the state of things, polemical journalism and theatre. (Remember, 'relevance' was one of that time's keywords, especially in the theatre.) Television and cinema couldn't work this rapidly or as tendentiously or as directly, and couldn't risk starting a project with an untried writer and no script.

It didn't occur to me to say no to this adventure; I rarely said no to anything in those days. I didn't think much about whether I was the sort of writer best-suited to this kind of work; I just knew I was being paid to write. But, if you weren't too sensitive, it was beneficial, because the pressures were intense and unusual. I learned what hell it could be trying to write a substantial piece, a full-length play, in a hurry. It also taught me the value and necessity of research in pursuing new ideas, and of detail, of reporting in its most basic sense. I discovered that this way of working, of finding out about the world and reflecting it, suited me better than a more cerebral or experimental approach. I'd hated the Robbe-Grillet, Duras and Sarraute method, which I found arid and dull, a dead-end. I also knew that a good writer

xviii

draws deeply on himself or herself, but that one can't go on writing and rewriting one's autobiography for ever.

It was both agreeable and awkward having to write for actors who had already been cast. As the range and limitations of those in the company became clear, I wrote for it, providing character and dialogue that suited the actors. I wrote for the director too, who might decide he wanted to set a scene here, or there, and could I please try and write it.

All this, feeling like a carpenter for hire, was excellent discipline. If someone wanted you to put up shelves here, or build a door there, then you did it. And why not? In the Joint Stock 'method', the democratic will of the company was sovereign, rather than that of the individual writer's imagination. It was a good experiment; and as I wrote to order, with the group supplying ideas, I liked to imagine that working in Hollywood would be like this, though presumably the pay would be better there. It was certainly useful preparation for writing films where, on the set, new dialogue and rewritten scenes are required instantly.

Unfortunately, the idea behind *Borderline* was impossible. It was using a method, journalism, as the tool for a different form, art or theatre. The result could only be external, sketchy, an impression. We knew the subject was there but we couldn't get at it, not from this far outside – it was too big, too vague – and not from the inside, either: we didn't know enough. A play is not an article in a newspaper. What did we think we could bring back, apart from the acceptance of our ignorance, and the knowledge that the British Empire had released forces that would transform much?

At least the research helped me begin to see the diversity and drama of the Asian community. But I knew I had to find a way of knitting ideas to specific characters, events and emotions, based on my own experience. I began to write *My Beautiful Laundrette*, which was, in many ways, a synthesis and extension of the plays which preceded it.

Indeed, all these plays were a setting-out of the themes that would absorb me for a long time, as if I were beginning to discover what my subject would be. A character from *The King and Me* – an idea I procured from a TV programme about a woman who was obsessed with Jim Reeves, and which I yoked to my own frustration and self-hatred about not being able to write – turned up in *London Kills Me*. The lives of the suburban couple Ted and Jean from *Birds of Passage* were extended in *The Buddha of Suburbia*, and the boys from *Outskirts* were the genesis of the boys in *My Beautiful Laundrette*.

I remember Evelyn Waugh saying in an interview that he envied Anthony Powell for being able to use the same characters in book after book instead of having to think up new aliases for what were basically the same people. Your characters don't leave you just because you've stopped writing about them; you can't help wanting to know what they might be doing after the duration of the play, film or book in which they appeared. This continuity, or what happens to people, interests me: in *Outskirts* the double time-scheme enables me to focus on this by binding two periods together, through a violent act in the context of unemployment and nationalism of the late 1970s, and the despair they caused.

This was also the context of *Birds of Passage*, a more naturalistic play, an old-fashioned play, in some ways. Since then, I haven't attempted another play. This is partly a matter of form rather than choice. I stopped being able to find a tone or style to accommodate my voice or themes. I didn't feel comfortable writing plays any more: I didn't know what sort of plays they should be; and the challenge of that doubt didn't stimulate me. It was strange, because for at least ten years all I wanted to do was write plays, and I took it for granted that a life in the theatre was the life for me.

Hanif Kureishi, London, 1991

THE KING AND ME

Characters

MARIE
NICOLA
BILL
M.C.

The King and Me was first performed at the Soho Poly Theatre, London, on 7 January 1980. The cast was as follows:

MARIE	Elaine Donnelly
NICOLA	Jean Trend
BILL	Mike Grady
M.C.	Eric Richard
Director	Antonia Bird
Designer	Louise Belson

Front room of a council flat. It is filled with Elvis paraphernalia.
Enter MARIE. *She is about thirty. She puts on an Elvis record as soon*
as she comes in. 'King Creole'. Her sister NICOLA *enters. She is about*
thirty-eight. She switches off the record.

NICOLA: Marie. (*Pause.*) Marie, well done love.

MARIE: Made it.

NICOLA: All right out there, was it?

MARIE: Yeah.

NICOLA: Marie.

MARIE: I hate it.

NICOLA: At least you got out.

MARIE: Don't go on. You sound like Bill.

NICOLA: He's right.

MARIE: I get out twice a week. I'm not the Prisoner of Zenda.

NICOLA: Both times you see that Elvis show.

MARIE: It's ugly out.

    (*She unpacks her shopping. One of the bags obviously contains*
    bottles. They clink together.)

NICOLA: Light refreshment?

    (MARIE *takes out a bottle of gin.*)

MARIE: Give your jaws a rest, Nicola. You know what it is.
    Tonight's the night, isn't it?

NICOLA: What night's that then?

MARIE: The big one. The biggest.

NICOLA: It's not Elvis's birthday again?

MARIE: You know it's not.

NICOLA: Is it the anniversary of his death? We won't have to wear
    black for a month, will we?

MARIE: He's come through the heats. He's in with a chance.
    Have you got a fag?

NICOLA: Have one of mine. (*Gives her one.*)

MARIE: It's the final of the competition.

NICOLA: Oh yeah.

MARIE: Don't pretend not to know.

5

NICOLA: That Elvis farce you been driving Bill crazy with all this time?

MARIE: You're being thick, Nicola. Cut it out. You and Bill should get together more. The rocks in your head would fit the holes in his.

NICOLA: Tell me . . . no, I want to know. What exactly will he be doing?

MARIE: We've got more chance than with the pools.

NICOLA: That's better than no chance at all. But what's he going in for?

MARIE: General Elvis knowledge and impersonation.

NICOLA: Your Bill can't sing.

MARIE: He doesn't have to warble, thank God. He mimes. He can do that.

NICOLA: Your Bill can't win that. (*Pause.*) Can he? Can he? (*Sadly.*) Oh Marie.

(MARIE *pours herself a drink.*)

MARIE: This is nice. I'll be celebrating or despairing tonight when the idiot gets home from it. One or the other. This stuff'll get me through. Come on Nicola. Want one now?

NICOLA: D'you need one?

MARIE: I feel like it. I don't need it. Come on love.

NICOLA: Na.

MARIE: Come on.

NICOLA: I've got to go up the PTA later. See your Vernon's teacher for you.

MARIE: Oh yeah.

NICOLA: You haven't said a lot about this impersonation.

MARIE: No.

NICOLA: Why not?

MARIE: He's ashamed, I think. He thinks I'm showing him up.

NICOLA: You are.

MARIE: No.

NICOLA: Grown man with two kids, pretending to be Presley.

MARIE: It's a chance to get away to Memphis.

(*Puts on 'Love Me Tender'. Moves to the music. Kicks off her shoes. Throws some of the kids' scattered toys into a corner.*)

6

You know . . . coming up here with yer shopping's like walking the gauntlet. There was one old bag who had her nose hanging out her door like a warty frankfurter. As I went past she started tut-tutting. You know how they do. Like a death rattle. Her false teeth doing the hokey-cokey. So I went back and gave her a mouthful. Guess what I said.

NICOLA: No.

MARIE: Go on.

NICOLA: You'd go in there one night and chuck acid in her face?

MARIE: How did you guess?

NICOLA: I'm clairvoyant.

MARIE: Someone should put a bomb under this estate.

NICOLA: You've turned people against you.

MARIE: We don't know anyone.

NICOLA: I do.

MARIE: They don't like you much. You put on airs.

NICOLA: You stink here. They think you're screwy. I reckon they've put their finger on something there.

MARIE: What's screwy about me?

NICOLA: No.

MARIE: Go on.

NICOLA: Well . . . you put your record-player out on the balcony at three o'clock in the morning and had Elvis on full that time.

MARIE: Oh, that.

NICOLA: That was bad enough.

MARIE: Shook them up nasty and cruel that night. We'd been playing cards. You'd gone home. You should have come back to see them when I was dancing out there. Lights coming on all around me. Them flushed out their flats like I'd started a fire in there – in their nighties and hairnets – one woman screaming, one geezer hanging off the fire-escape in his thermal underwear.

NICOLA: Who was that?

MARIE: He came up and hit Bill with a cricket-bat.

NICOLA: That's right.

MARIE: And there they all were, standing on their balconies – watching me dance.

7

NICOLA: Naked.

MARIE: It was a hot night. God . . . I felt so . . . delicious. I felt like I was on 'Sunday Night at the London Palladium'. I should have charged a viewing fee. The law had a laugh.

NICOLA: I'm glad I wasn't there.

MARIE: I remember when Bill and I had the bike. It's gone rusty standing outside now. And we can't afford the parts. We'd go out on a Sunday.

NICOLA: I remember.

MARIE: In a pack. Down to the coast. (MARIE *kisses a picture of Elvis.*) It was a night like that.

NICOLA: You know . . .

MARIE: What?

NICOLA: I can't stand that greasy Elvis with the Torrey Canyon smeared over his head.

MARIE: He's the king.

NICOLA: He's –

MARIE: Are they behaving themselves?

NICOLA: That Vernon's a real beast. I've told you before. Lisa-Marie's all right. She's placid.

MARIE: What's Vernon done?

NICOLA: Gone and jabbed holes in my new chairs with me knitting needles.

MARIE: (*Proud*) Sounds like his style.

NICOLA: My love, listen. You can have them back in a minute. I've told them my place ain't their home. But they prefer me to you. If they stay with me too often –

MARIE: I said I'll come down for them.

NICOLA: What time?

MARIE: When I've trimmed Bill's sideburns and got him off to the town hall . . . oh and I've got to finish off his costume and – (*Jumps about delightedly.*) Wee . . . Jesus Nicky, my love. Two tickets to Memphis, Tennessee when we win tonight. Bill and me'll get ripped good and proper out there.

NICOLA: You'll have to come home.

MARIE: For six months after we'll be high as kites. Remember –

NICOLA: When?

MARIE: We came back from seeing the king in Vegas. It ripped

8

me that time. I didn't need nothing nor no one. Vegas. Vegas.

NICOLA: Your Bill doesn't look anything like Elvis.

MARIE: What?

NICOLA: He's the last person to impersonate Elvis. I'm surprised you married him.

MARIE: Did it for a dare.

NICOLA: You. (*Pause.*) He looks like Alan Ladd.

MARIE: What?

NICOLA: He looks more like Alan Ladd than Elvis. He'll need plastic surgery if he's going to win. What happens if he doesn't?

MARIE: Don't – I'll explode or something. Blow up. Things can't stay the same.

NICOLA: They always do.

MARIE: Couldn't stand it.

NICOLA: What would you do?

MARIE: Make something happen.

NICOLA: How?

MARIE: I'd have to.

NICOLA: How?

MARIE: I couldn't stand it.

(MARIE *puts on 'His Latest Flame' by Elvis. Dances, more vigorously this time, since it's an up-tempo number.* NICOLA *shouts at her through the music.*)

NICOLA: Turn it down, Marie!

MARIE: What?

NICOLA: Marie. Blimey!

MARIE: What is it? (MARIE *snaps off the music.*) What is it?

NICOLA: That's what I was going to ask. I reckon they'll lock you up.

MARIE: Why?

NICOLA: They'll cart you away if you keep on going into them trances.

MARIE: Why?

NICOLA: Oh Marie . . . because it's out of this world, some of the things you do.

MARIE: I didn't know they'd made dancing a crime.

9

NICOLA: I didn't mean that.

MARIE: Then me Elvis collection's the first sign of madness is it now?

NICOLA: Our mother had hobbies . . . she would –

MARIE: Spit it out, love.

NICOLA: It's the way you go about it. Not letting anything else interfere. Just loving Elvis the way you do: more than anything else. You see that Elvis show twice a week.

MARIE: It's a great show.

NICOLA: It might be. If Christ was tap-dancing with John the Baptist on the harmonium I wouldn't want to see it that often.

MARIE: You. What d'you think I get up to in there, twice a week?

NICOLA: I wouldn't be surprised if you peed yer pants every time.

MARIE: I have done that an' all. (*They have a laugh.*) No, come on. What do I do then?

NICOLA: Must be something special.

MARIE: It's gorgeous Nicky. I look forward to it all week. And then I get in there, in the dark, all on me own, with a box of chocolates –

NICOLA: And a small bottle of –

MARIE: Yeah. It's a real thrill. I have delicious thoughts. It's like showing films in me mind. Like day-dreams; wishes come true. No, more like films really.

NICOLA: All about Presley?

MARIE: Mostly. Him and me. Together.

NICOLA: His films. I've seen 'em. Those films.

MARIE: Mine are everything. I should be a film director. I should be Farrah Fawcett Majors. Some of them are sexy.

NICOLA: Are they?

MARIE: I do anything in them. Everything.

NICOLA: Does he always have that guitar dangling round his neck?

MARIE: And they're different every time. Just me and the king, meeting in different places: restaurants, pubs, beaches, clubs, casinos. It's the best time I have, in that theatre. I don't think I can explain it. Nothing'll stop me going. (*Pause.*)

NICOLA: I better get back before your boy has me wallpaper down.

MARIE: Yes, okay.

NICOLA: You like your peace of an afternoon.

MARIE: Yeah, I do. I've got to finish Bill's outfit. (*She holds it up.*) What do you think?

NICOLA: I don't know Marie.

MARIE: Come on.

NICOLA: Drag show?

MARIE: Three months it's taken me.

NICOLA: Has it? Come down and get those kids off my back.

MARIE: I will.

NICOLA: I know you. (*Pause.*) You don't have to work and you don't wanna take care of them. What do you want?

MARIE: I want –

NICOLA: A good kick up the arse would do you. Jolt you.

MARIE: I can't get worked up over the kids. I try to. Don't people notice that about kids?

NICOLA: What?

MARIE: How boring they are. Sometimes I want to go mad. I want to go wild. Really fucking wild.

NICOLA: Marie don't swear!
    (*The front door bangs.*)

MARIE: It's him. Be nice to him Nicky. Encourage him about tonight.

NICOLA: He can't win.

MARIE: For me Nicky.

NICOLA: Marie!
    (*Enter* BILL, *Marie's husband, still in his ticket-collector's uniform but with various 'Ted' additions.*)

BILL: All right Nicola? (*To* MARIE.) How are you love?

NICOLA: I'm just off.

BILL: You've always got time for a cup of tea and a biscuit (*Smells her*) – and half a bottle of gin.

NICOLA: Not me. I've got to –

BILL: Glad you been up here this afternoon. Marie likes a bit of company of an afternoon.

NICOLA: (*Indicates picture of Elvis*) She's always got company. She's got Mr Elvis the Pelmet.

BILL: You're right about that.

MARIE: Bill. You've got to start getting ready.

NICOLA: Got to get in yer Liberace costume have you Bill?

BILL: Look – don't mock the terrified.

NICOLA: Whatever you do tonight, don't do your back in again. I don't want to have to go through all that massage and hot-water bottle treatment again.

MARIE: Nicola!

NICOLA: All right Elvis – I expect I'll see you tomorrow.

BILL: I'll be down for a chat.

NICOLA: Right. Here – Bill.

BILL: Yeah?

NICOLA: Why don't you give us a bit of an advance viewing like?

BILL: Eh?

NICOLA: Go on Bill. Shake it around for us, like you're going to tonight. Go on.

BILL: Na. Gotta get going.

MARIE: Leave him alone, Nicola.

BILL: (*To* MARIE) We're only having a laugh.

NICOLA: He's got to save it up for later, has he?

MARIE: That's right. He has.

NICOLA: His whole life's been like that.

BILL: You could be right there. (*Laughs.*)

NICOLA: Good luck Billy boy.

BILL: Ta love.

NICOLA: I mean it. Don't rupture yourself. Not over a bit of fun.

BILL: I'll be careful.

MARIE: (*Irritated*) Bye Nicola. Thanks for the helpful advice.

NICOLA: Pleasure.

(*Exit* NICOLA. *The mood changes.*)

BILL: Where are my kids?

MARIE: Eh?

BILL: Are they downstairs?

MARIE: Bill.

BILL: Is that where they are?

MARIE: Yeah.

BILL: Don't you think I like to see them when I get in?

MARIE: They get under your feet.

BILL: It's the only time I do want to see them and they're not here. (*He attempts to kiss her.*)

MARIE: You're in me light. Must finish this. No time.

BILL: You.

MARIE: How did it go today?

BILL: Same.

MARIE: Same what?

BILL: Same old shit.

MARIE: I'm interested.

BILL: You are today. Been out?
(*She nods.*)
Really?

MARIE: Picked up an Elvis souvenir book.

BILL: Good.

MARIE: Nothing in it I haven't read a thousand times. They think we don't know. They think we're stupid.

BILL: Glad you got out.

MARIE: Oh shut it.

BILL: Hey Marie, I'm bloody nervy about tonight, you know. I haven't felt this shaky since I took me O levels.

MARIE: You didn't get them.

BILL: Oh don't rub me up the wrong way. You went to that paying school and all you can think about is America's answer to Cliff Richard.

MARIE: Careful.

BILL: Sorry.

MARIE: Now chat about something nice.

BILL: Good last night, weren't it?

MARIE: Look Bill, you've got to get ready.

BILL: It surprises me. Still ace, ain't it, after all this time. It's one thing we're good at. And you're best on your back.

MARIE: Let me concentrate!

BILL: You know, when we're at it –

MARIE: Christ you're on stage in –

BILL: Am I?

MARIE: Yes.

BILL: Do you think I'll go through with it?

MARIE: Yes. (*Pause.*) Yes.

13

BILL: When I'm steaming away like the clappers, giving it all I got, I often get wondering: what is she thinking about? I don't like to stop and ask, like, so I wondered . . .

MARIE: What are you saying?

BILL: I'd like to know. Otherwise I don't think I'll be able to perform tonight.

MARIE: I don't think about anything much.

BILL: Your mind's blank?

MARIE: No.

BILL: What then?

MARIE: Well . . . I think about the king. All right? I think you're him.

BILL: (*Taking the costume from her*) What, every time?

MARIE: I can't think of a time when Elvis wasn't on my mind. (BILL *puts the jacket on. Preens himself.*)

BILL: Our kids got started when you were thinking about Presley?

MARIE: Bill, what do you think about?

BILL: It's funny. I think about the king too.

MARIE: (*Laughing*) Come on, you've got to run through the number. (*She goes to put the record on.*)

BILL: Now?

MARIE: I'm your agent. Your Mickey Most.

BILL: I tell you, I'll be glad when it's over tonight. I can't take much more of your attention. I'm not used to it.

MARIE: Come on.

BILL: Have I really got time?

MARIE: You're going without your dinner.

BILL: Let me fix me hair.
(*She watches him as he takes great care with his hair.*)

MARIE: (*Half to him, mostly to herself*) I don't know why I'm wearing me nerves down over this. You aren't going to win, you big prick. You ain't got a hope. You're not crazy to win. But you must win, Billy. If you don't –

BILL: What are you saying?

MARIE: I was saying I don't know what'll happen if you don't win tonight.

BILL: Nothing'll happen.

14

MARIE: Right.

BILL: We'll be disappointed. And we'll go back to being just like we are now.

MARIE: Will we? (*She puts on the record.* BILL *refuses to respond.*) Bill!

BILL: I don't know, Marie. I feel so daft. Five years ago I wouldn't have. But what with me slipped disc and the kids and everything. I'm worried that someone from work might see me. I won't live it down at work.

MARIE: You've got to make your movements smoother. The way you're doing it now, the judges'll think you've caught a touch of the DTs.

BILL: I'll be well-oiled tonight.

MARIE: Everything'll change if we can get to Memphis. We'll never save that kind of money again.

BILL: We can't hardly afford a pot of Brylcream between us.

MARIE: Are you ready for your questions? Are you?

BILL: Yes . . . right . . . shoot.

MARIE: Who sold more records than the king?

BILL: Bing Crosby. And the Beatles.

MARIE: Good. What's his parents' names?

BILL: Easy. Vernon and Gladys.

MARIE: Good. Now who did the king drive trucks for?

BILL: Er . . .

MARIE: Come on.

BILL: Crown –

MARIE: Come on.

BILL: Crown Electric Company – Thirty-five dollars a week.

MARIE: All right. They're the ones you had trouble with.

BILL: I'd like you to come tonight, love.

MARIE: You know me.

BILL: I'd like you to be there to urge me on.

MARIE: I've done all I can for you.

BILL: You know what I think? You'll go bonkers staying here all the time. It's imprisonment.

MARIE: I reckon I've got one of the best collections in England. I'm making an index of all the things I've got. I'll be all right. I always am.

15

BILL: Will you be talking to Elvis tonight?

MARIE: What did you say?

BILL: Open yer ear-holes.

MARIE: Just go will you?

BILL: I've gone. There's something else.

MARIE: What?

BILL: I want the kids to sleep here tonight.

MARIE: I'll bring them up.

(BILL *thrusts the costume in her face*.)

BILL: Kiss it for good luck.

(*She does so; rubs it against her cheek*.)

Get packed girl. And don't forget me sun-tan oil and
Bermuda shorts.

MARIE: Win for Christ's sake Billy. Give it to them, boy!

BILL: I will, girl! (*Pause*.) It's hard on the kids, all this.

MARIE: Don't I deserve to be happy?

BILL: Yeah, course. But –

MARIE: You better go.

BILL: Right. I'll do me best for you, girl. I do love you. Do you
love me Marie?

(*Pause*.)

MARIE: Bill. Cut them to fucking pieces.

BILL: Yeah. I will.

(*He goes.*

MARIE *pours a drink. She goes to her Elvis mirror – kisses it. On
with 'In The Ghetto'. And as the lights fade she raises her glass to
toast Bill's coming success*.)

MARIE: Memphis!

(*Blackout*.)

SCENE TWO

The Elvis Show.
*A curtain can be drawn across the previous set and it might be
interesting if we could see* MARIE *through it, sitting drinking in the
background. Various asides and jokes during this scene could be
improvised both in rehearsal and during the actual playing of it.*

16

Enter M.C., *in an orange suit, etc. Laughing.*

M.C.: (*Indicating to the wings*) And I hope he makes it back from hospital in time for the presentation. See them legs? Last time I saw legs like that they were down the end of the garden with runner beans growing up them! No, seriously, my wife's got legs like that – and we put her in front of the fire and hang washing on them. Careful with that stretcher lads! (*Pause.*) Well, ladies and gentlemen, the show must go on. And our next contestant in this special 'Elvis for Memphis' night is – Bill! Come on Bill!
(*Enter* BILL *in his amazing costume, fumbling and nervous and dazed by the lights.*)
Over here Bill. On the spot. Good lad. Now, let's have your full name.

BILL: Bill Bird.

M.C.: No need to shout, Bill. What do your friends call you Bill?

BILL: Bill.

M.C.: Right. And where are you from?

BILL: Catford.

M.C.: Billy Bird from Catford! What about that then sweethearts? Now, now, we don't want to be taking any cheap trills out of this boy. Now Bill, tell everyone out there what you do for a living. Let's hope we can keep this one legal. What do you do, Bill?

BILL: I'm a ticket-collector. On the Underground. London Transport.

M.C.: And what do you do when you're not collecting tickets?

BILL: Eh?

M.C.: I mean, don't you have any hobbies?

BILL: No.

M.C.: You don't learn languages? Or make wine in the garage?

BILL: No.

M.C.: Don't you support football?

BILL: Yeah. I got a team. QPR. They're my team.

M.C.: Thought I recognized you! Seen you on Match of the Day chucking a bog roll at Liverpool's goalkeeper. Well Bill, just before your big moment isn't there anyone out there in the audience you'd like to say hallo to? Haven't you got your girlfriend or your wife out there?

BILL: No.

M.C.: No? Not even your mum?

BILL: No. She's dead. She died of –

M.C.: (*Quickly*) All right Bill, I'm sure the lads'll be right behind you. (*To the audience*.) And looking at some of them lads I wouldn't want them behind me! One more thing Bill. Better check your pelvis is in good working order. Let's have a preview.

BILL: Eh?

M.C.: Go on.

(BILL *gives us a pelvic wiggle*.)

Fine, fine. And let's have a look at that sneer, that Elvis lip.

(BILL *gives us the Elvis sneer*.)

It all looks fully-oiled to me!

BILL: I am, mate!

(M.C. *stands away*.)

M.C.: Are you ready Bill? For tonight's the night, and the stage is yours – Bill Bird from Catford with 'Blue Suede Shoes' – Mr Elvis Presley!

(BILL *does the mime to 'Blue Suede Shoes'*. M.C. *comes back on*. BILL *exhausted*.)

M.C.: And let's have a round of applause for a fine and fast attempt from – Brian.

BILL: Bill.

M.C.: Now Bill, please relax. Take your time. I'm going to give you four questions. You have five seconds to answer each one. Are you ready Bill? Now relax. (*Pause*.) What is Elvis's surname?

BILL: Eh? Er . . . ahhh . . .

M.C.: Two seconds Billy.

BILL: Presley. Elvis Presley.

M.C.: Well done. A little slow out of the traps there, but he made it up on the home-straight, didn't he sweethearts? Still, haven't we got a good boy here. We don't know yet how the judges have marked his card, but I've got a feeling he'll be up with the big ones. Now Billy. (*Pause*.) Who did Elvis drive trucks for?

BILL: Crown Electric Company – Thirty-five dollars a week.

M.C.: Absolutely right. With a nice little flourish at the end. No extra marks for that of course. No nearer Memphis, Billy. Now just turn round Bill and show our punters the back of that superb costume. Did you make it yourself?

BILL: Na. My wife made it. Marie.

M.C.: Oh, you have got a little trouble and strife.
(BILL *nods*.)
And how long did it take her?

BILL: Three months.

M.C.: Three months to sew on thirty-six studs – amazing! (*Pause*.) Now Bill, the next question's coming right up. What size socks did Elvis take?

BILL: Eh?

M.C.: I'm sorry – I didn't mean that. What size shoes did Elvis wear?

BILL: Seven! No – eight!

M.C.: Good answer! Sorry about the confusion. Still, we like to keep our competitors on their toes. Now, I want you to relax Billy. I want you to concentrate the full force of your mind on the next question. The one at the bottom of the page. This is not a trick question. There are no trick questions, ladies and gentlemen. I want you, Bill, to think of you and your wife Mary –

BILL: Marie.

M.C.: Marie . . . strolling down Elvis Presley Boulevard towards the wrought-iron gates of Gracelands as they open . . . just for you and your wife . . . Take your time Billy. (*Pause*.) In what year did Elvis release 'Suspicious Minds'?

BILL: 1970.

M.C.: Thank you for a great effort. But 1969 would have been a better guess. Sorry Bill. Now let's have a round of applause. Ladies and Gentlemen. It must seem obvious to you as it does to me that Billy has star potential. It'll probably stay star-potential . . . you never know. Off you go Billy. (*As* BILL *goes off*.) Don't give up your day-time job my son. Keep punching them tickets. And we'll see you later, at the presentation.

(BILL *has gone*.)
I tell you, if we get any more like that, we'll be holding the
presentation in Charing Cross Hospital. (*Returns centre
stage*.) And now for our next contestant.
(*Blackout*.)

SCENE THREE

As Scene One.
Enter BILL *in his costume. He's carrying a record in a plastic bag,
under his arm. He has received a black eye.*
BILL: All right flower?
(*She sits there, drumming her fingers*.)
MARIE: I was starting to unpack your Bermuda shorts. I was
thinking you'd gone to Memphis without me. It's the sort of
thing you'd do.
BILL: Couldn't get a bus here. Had to walk all the way back. Ran
into a bit of nuisance.
MARIE: Eh?
BILL: With four little punks. They wanted to take the piss outta
my sequins.
MARIE: What happened?
BILL: Sorted them out, didn't I?
MARIE: You could have changed. Why did you have to come
sweating back in that costume? Did you have to go out in
something that took me three months to do?
BILL: Shut up about the rag! I had to get out of all that. Couldn't
stand it. The humiliation.
MARIE: Eh? (*Pause*.) What's that under your arm?
BILL: (*Sniffs*) Deodorant.
MARIE: Don't kid me tonight.
BILL: Christ!
MARIE: What is it?
(*He gives her the record. She looks at it and throws it down*.)
Got it.
BILL: I know that don't I?
MARIE: What you hawk it up six flights for then?

BILL: I won it.

MARIE: What?

BILL: I won it. I couldn't turn it down could I? I couldn't give it
back to Raving Rupert and say: sorry mate, my cow wife's
worn out eight copies and we've just started on our ninth. I
couldn't tell him to stuff fifth prize up his arse!

MARIE: Finished?

BILL: Yes.

MARIE: (*False jollity*) Hey Bill, God said unto Moses come forth
and you will win the world. He came fifth and won a teapot.

BILL: (*Furious*) You should have been there tonight, Marie!
Every Elvis had his wife of his bird or both cheering him on.
It probably would have made a lot of difference. I mean it,
doll.

MARIE: You know what your problem is?

BILL: What's my problem?

MARIE: You're the spitting image of Alan Ladd. The more I look
at you the more you look like Alan Ladd.

BILL: (*Slightly puzzled*) It might have made a difference if you'd
been scowling from the front row. Only you never go out.

MARIE: (*Furious too*) Just tell me what there is out there that's
worth going out for!

BILL: All right, all right. I buggered one question right up,
Marie.

MARIE: Don't tell me we went down the toilet because of a cinch.
What was it? What's Elvis's surname?

BILL: Jesus! Jesus! I'll rip this thing in a minute. (*He goes to rip his
jacket.*) And then I'll smash this place up. Your refuge. Like
I did before.

MARIE: No. Tell me what it was. Go on. Gob it out.

BILL: What year did the king release 'Suspicious Minds'?

MARIE: You idiot.

BILL: I know it don't I? I mean, I know what it is but my brain
got blocked. I was nervous. *You* got me all worked up, I was
thinking of you sitting here, and I said 1970.

MARIE: In 1969 he released 'Suspicious Minds' and in 1970 he
put out 'The Wonder of You'. On RCA.

BILL: I hit the target with the others Marie. I was up there, cruising, when we got to the impersonations. If only I could have had it. My back played up. We'd be half-way to Memphis by now.

MARIE: I'm half-way outta my brain. That's something.

BILL: Marie . . . sometimes I think we were wrong to set such store by it. We built it up – in our minds, over the last few months. You were relying on it much more than you thought.

MARIE: What about the impersonation? We practised every night. For Christ's sake, how did you manage to cock it up?

BILL: Cock it up? I didn't do too bad. The swine said I had star potential. That's not too bad for a beginner. Don't forget who I was pitting myself up against. Old pros. They were at it when I was slashing seats up at the Odeon. They made me look like Jim Reeves.

MARIE: I've had enough of you Billy.

BILL: Let's go to bed.

MARIE: I won't be able to sleep.

BILL: Think about Elvis – you'll soon drop off. (*Pause.*) I've got to go to work early. Come on.

MARIE: I want to hear some music.

BILL: Not now.

MARIE: Yes.

BILL: Me head's throbbing. And it's too late for all that.

MARIE: If it's too late, you're too old.

BILL: You'll wake the – the kids are here aren't they?

MARIE: Your children are at home and completely quiet for once.

BILL: (*Laughing*) You haven't gassed them? (*Pause.*) Don't wake them. Don't wake the neighbours. Jesus I couldn't face that docker from downstairs with his karate kicks.

MARIE: I want to hear something. And I want to dance.

BILL: What do you want to do that for?

MARIE: I need a good time, I think. It's been so long I can't remember what it's like. I've got to get rid of something – in me.

BILL: You can bloody do your dances all day. There's no one here then to stand in your way. You get rid of my kids with your sister. And you don't do a thing!

MARIE: I do!

22

BILL: You just prance around like a blue-arsed fly. Wearing out the carpet all afternoon.

MARIE: What?

BILL: Your Nicola told me.

MARIE: What did she tell you?

BILL: She's caught you at it. She said you're like some kind of person who has fits. Epi . . . epilep –

MARIE: My God!

BILL: Well, that's what she said to me. When I'm at work you're always dancing around, chatting to yourself.

MARIE: At the same time?

BILL: Sometimes you have to be truthful Marie. Is she telling lies about you?

MARIE: I don't talk to myself. I talk to the king if I talk to anyone. I'm not a maniac, I'm not that, Bill.

BILL: Well, that's it then. You've admitted it. You're talking and dancing away every afternoon, like a mad person.

MARIE: You've been getting together, you and her. Your big flapping gobs puking it out about me. I can see you, on her sofa, eating her cake. (*Mimicking.*) What does that Marie do? She's barmy, jumping around for hours like a jack-in-the-box, chatting away to a dead singer. Have another piece of cake – no I won't – go on – oh all right – I can't do a thing with her . . . (*Pause.*) She's a bitch. I can see that now. You're a bastard, Bill.

BILL: I don't know what's happening to you. I really don't. It's got to stop.

MARIE: No.

BILL: It must.

MARIE: No.

(*He rips off the jacket. She takes it.*)

Leave it. I'll go mad.

BILL: You're a strait-jacket case.

MARIE: Leave everything alone.

BILL: You're a padded-cell number.

MARIE: Open your bloody ears to what I have to say. I want to listen to the king and I want to dance. I have to dance or else I'll explode.

BILL: Why, for Christ sake, why all the exploding?

MARIE: What's wrong with what I do? You explode every Friday night, don't you?

BILL: Well . . .

MARIE: Last week them teds dragged you back, yelling and sicking over the furniture. Wearing your boots in bed, ripping up the continental quilt.

BILL: You bloody love the king. You don't just like him. Our bedroom's a shrine to Presley. I bet if you had him on one side and me on the other – I know which way you'd turn.

MARIE: You're marvellous.

BILL: We've got to talk about what's going on.

MARIE: You just realized all this?

BILL: I'm lost, you get me? I don't know what I'd hate most. A flesh-and-blood geezer from the betting-shop in here for an afternoon bang and a bit of a suck. Or this stuff with the king. At least with a real geezer I'd know where I was. I could take an afternoon off from work and stick a knife in him. That'd be right. But I mean, this stuff, it's too weird –

MARIE: Don't think about it.

BILL: I do. All the time.

MARIE: Don't talk about it then.

BILL: I will. The king's done nothing for us. The council have done more. Elvis hasn't lifted a finger. We're still in this muck – no money, them kids, no nothing. He never even replied when you used to write to him every week.

MARIE: He must have had millions of letters.

BILL: He had no excuses. He wasn't dead then. He never even came to England to see us.

MARIE: What about when –

BILL: What?

MARIE: He sent one of his pink Cadillacs to England for his fans to touch.

BILL: The car ran over your foot. He tried to put you in a wheelchair.

MARIE: It wasn't his fault. None of this is.

BILL: It's too late now to put up your umbrella. You've been pissed on.

MARIE: Shut up will you?

BILL: Don't wake them brats.

MARIE: I like dancing.

BILL: I know.

MARIE: Do you know what it's like to have a bit of a jig . . . so you feel yourself drifting away, like you're hypnotized or drugged or something? That feeling we'd get when we'd come back from a long trip on the bike.

BILL: Marie. You've got to understand. I feel it coming on.

MARIE: What?

BILL: We're . . . old people.

MARIE: Already?

BILL: Not like your mum and dad in age. But you know what I'm getting at. Set – we are. No more big chances. The pattern's made now. You've got to get settled Marie. You've got to start making an effort.

MARIE: Effort? What effort?

BILL: Some . . . effort.

MARIE: You haven't made an effort in years, have you?

BILL: I've shagged myself out trying.

MARIE: When?

BILL: I stuck at those evening classes a whole year. I went every week. Didn't miss one.

MARIE: No.

BILL: Wanted to change it. I still want to. You can help. You could better yourself.

MARIE: I couldn't.

BILL: Anyone can. You're clever.

MARIE: I won't do anything like that.

BILL: It's a question of patience. In nine years you could have a University degree like that woman in the paper –

MARIE: Too long. I'm always waiting. Either for you to get home. Or for you to go out. I've looked at those kids till I had sore eyes waiting for them to grow up.

BILL: If we work . . . together . . . like we did on the bike in the past. We worked on that and we went on. We can get off the estate. There's nice places for the kids to play.

MARIE: All these people will stay here if we go.

25

BILL: They don't matter to us.

MARIE: No. Someone else'll move in.

BILL: And they'll bow down and kiss the mouldy floor-boards in gratitude. Like we did.

MARIE: They'll learn.

BILL: We'll be away. I'll make the new place nice. You can make . . . curtains. We can better ourselves. The opportunity's there. Only you've got to give up Elvis.

MARIE: You're being silly, saying that.

BILL: You're too old. And he's rotted in the ground by now. He played with guns, and got bloated; when he sweated, little bits of pill came out his pores.

MARIE: Watch your dirty mouth, Bill.

BILL: They're making fools of us.

MARIE: You're my fool.

BILL: We're not getting anywhere . . . in our lives.

MARIE: That's not my fault.

BILL: He's holding us back.

MARIE: Don't be daft. You've ruined us. Do more overtime.

BILL: Jesus.

MARIE: Get another job.

BILL: What would I be working for? More records, more pictures of Elvis and Priscilla?

MARIE: I'm fond of him, you see. And I can't help that now.
(BILL *rips down a picture*.)
Stop it!

BILL: I'm going to do damage in a minute, I mean it!

MARIE: I won't be changed by you.

BILL: Marie.

MARIE: Do you remember what we used to say to our geriatric friends when they wouldn't come out: never too old to rock and roll. Never too old to love Elvis.
(*He goes to her. She turns.*)
Bill.

BILL: Please.

MARIE: You're in front of my eyes.

BILL: What?

MARIE: Bill. Every time I close my eyes you're in the picture.

26

BILL: (*Sarcastic*) Oh sorry.

MARIE: I can't seem to . . . get clear, Bill.

BILL: I don't know if I can –

MARIE: I'll be all right if you want to go to bed. You must be exhausted, with what you've done.

BILL: Yeah.

MARIE: I don't need no noise. You won't catch me on the balcony. I can hear the tunes in my head. If I close my eyes I can make the pictures myself. I'm a human cinema.

BILL: You're three cinemas.

MARIE: Careful.

BILL: Marie . . .

(*He moves around the flat, ripping down the pictures and putting all the stuff in a big plastic dustbin bag.*)

MARIE: (*Eyes closed*) What are you doing?

BILL: Everything's changing.

MARIE: Bill.

BILL: Can't you hear it all changing?

MARIE: What will I have to look forward to?

BILL: The rest of your life. We can work. The king's finished. See? He's gone.

MARIE: (*Crying*) What are you doing?

(*He goes outside with the bag. Re-enters.*)

What are you doing now?

BILL: No.

MARIE: What?

BILL: It's done now.

MARIE: Why?

BILL: Jesus, I'm beginning to feel really clean. Don't you feel better already? I can feel myself getting stronger. We're on the way up.

MARIE: Am I allowed to have a bit of a dance when I want?

BILL: 'Course you can. Not when you're on your own. I'll get your sister to keep an eye on you. And I'll buy you some records by Elton John.

MARIE: I just like the king's music.

BILL: He hasn't done us any favours. So he's out. (*Pause.*) My back hurts. Can you rub my back or something. I've done

27

something to it. I feel like an old man (*Pause*.) Marie.
(*Pause*.) Marie. You can open your eyes now.
(*Blackout*.)

OUTSKIRTS

Characters

DEL
BOB
MAUREEN
MUM
JULIA

A play in twelve scenes set over twelve years.

Outskirts was first performed at The Royal Shakespeare Company's Warehouse Theatre, London, on 28 April 1981. The cast was as follows:

DEL	David Bamber
BOB	Tony Guilfoyle
MAUREEN	Illona Linthwaite
MUM	Marjorie Yates
JULIA	Tilly Vosburgh

SCENE ONE

The past. The waste-ground. It is beginning to get dark. DEL *is already there, shifting about, as he restlessly awaits his friend. Off-stage there is the sound of rotten timber splitting.*

DEL: What's that? What's happening out there? (*Pause.*) That you then, Bobby boy? That you? (*Pause.*) Or what?

BOB: (*Off*) No.

DEL: Bobby? (*Pause.*) Oh come on. It's bin like being on the moon up here, hanging on. It's windy.

BOB: You're windy. You've got the wind up. (*Pause.*) Just smashed me whole spine, practically. Leg's jammed through an old door you put here . . . deliberately. Now I'll have to walk round with it . . . (*Pulls. More splitting.*) . . . rest of me life. I'll never turn out for the Palace now.

DEL: You'll be all right in the Second Eleven.

BOB: With a ripped-off leg?

DEL: No one'll notice.

(BOB *comes on.*)

BOB: Hey. Don't give me that eye.

DEL: Didn't she get you a watch, with green stamps. I chose it. You could look at it now and then. I've bin waiting.

(BOB *hits him.*)

What's that for?

BOB: Leave out the backchat, Del.

DEL: God.

BOB: Del, I can't hang round now.

DEL: What's cooking tonight then?

BOB: It's on. All charging ahead.

DEL: Yeah?

BOB: I've set it. (BOB *walks off.*)

DEL: Where you gone?

BOB: See yer.

DEL: Bobby.

BOB: Don't get worried.

DEL: Tramps up here on the moon.

33

BOB: Must get back.

DEL: Bobby.

BOB: Del, she's in a mood. She's waiting for me.

DEL: Your mum in a mood?

BOB: Tonight, you know, we've had our tea, and after she pulls herself half-way up that step-ladder to the attic.

DEL: What's she doing?

BOB: Going to come down with the golf-clubs me dad left. And cane me arse.

DEL: Eh? Them rotted clubs? What about that ol' gypo we sold them to that time, over the allotments?

BOB: Quick as a flash you're on to me meaning.

DEL: Jesus, you'll be in trouble.

BOB: Don't tell me.

DEL: Well I wouldn't wanna be in your arse.

BOB: Who would, right?

DEL: Jesus wept.

BOB: (*Going*) By nine she'll be off like a dream in front of the telly. I'll be out soon as the first snore –

DEL: Where then?

BOB: Up the bomb-site.

DEL: Bit special.

BOB: Yeah. In two hours or so.

DEL: Right.

BOB: See ya.

DEL: Bob.

BOB: What?

DEL: Quick, gi's a fag then.
      (BOB *takes one from behind his ear*.)
      Another one of yer mum's?

BOB: You bet.

DEL: She'll –

BOB: Don't tell me. (*He runs off*.)

DEL: (*Pauses a moment. Lights up*.) Yeah. Right.
      (DEL *runs off in the opposite direction*.)

The present – twelve years later. BOB *enters, his arms full of beers. He goes off. Returns with more beers. He's singing to himself.*

His wife MAUREEN *comes on. She's carrying an overnight bag with an overcoat folded over her arm. She watches* BOB.

BOB: Hallo, lovely. Ready to go then?

MAUREEN: Yes.

BOB: Want me to phone for a cab?

MAUREEN: No. I've done that. (*Pause.*) He'll be a minute. On his way.

BOB: Jesus. When you think about it, it's the first time we've been apart since we got married.

MAUREEN: It is. It is.
     (*They hug.*)
     Will you finish the ironing without burning right through the glass-topped table? The nylon shirts and them other things, you just have to –

BOB: It's okay. I know all about that. (*He goes off.*)

MAUREEN: Where have you gone? I've got to ask something. (*She puts her overcoat on.*)

BOB: (*Off*) Hold on to yer horses. (*He brings on more booze.*)

MAUREEN: What's that?

BOB: What?

MAUREEN: All that?

BOB: Few drinks, eh?

MAUREEN: You're not going to –

BOB: 'Course not, 'course not.

MAUREEN: Try not to go berserk, Bo-Bo. Not now we've gone mad treating ourselves with that carpet out your mum's insurance money. The pile hasn't –

BOB: Settles in its own time.

MAUREEN: Yeah. You know, it seems . . . going away, and that. Bob, try and use the time.

BOB: You're making too much of a big thing out of this.

MAUREEN: I mustn't. All right.

BOB: Just enjoy it.

MAUREEN: Yes, it's only a weekend away.

BOB: Weekend?

MAUREEN: What?

BOB: You said – oh make up yer mind love – a long weekend, you said. You did say that. I should have taped it. And I've gone to all this trouble.

MAUREEN: You said, in the kitchen, it'll feel like a long weekend. You were so excited.

BOB: I thought it would be four days or something.

MAUREEN: You'll have your fun.

BOB: All right.

MAUREEN: Jesus God, I didn't say I was off on a world cruise.

BOB: Hold on. Just coming back. (BOB *goes off. He returns with a crate of beer.*) Won't Del want something after his journey, eh?

MAUREEN: Why, where's he coming from?

BOB: Islington, or somewhere.
       (*Pause. She smiles at him.*)

MAUREEN: If you could see your little face now.

BOB: That rash come up?

MAUREEN: You're holding your face in.

BOB: Go, just go!

MAUREEN: Like a naughty boy. It's like jelly in a mould. You'll go mad when the door slams behind me.

BOB: Not true.

MAUREEN: I bet your funny balls in their bean-bag have gone tight, eh? Let's have a look.

BOB: Get off me. (*Pause.*) You set this weekend up. You said it's me who needs the rest.

MAUREEN: You certainly do, you see; you do.
       (*Front door bell rings.*)

BOB: That's your cab. (*Pause.*) Natural to be a bit excited.

MAUREEN: That's why you look so unnatural, Bob.

BOB: How's that then?

MAUREEN: This morning I saw you on the bed, no clothes on, drying your hair.

BOB: Where were you?

MAUREEN: I spied you through the crack of the bedroom door. You moved about the room, sat down, got up –

BOB: Big deal.

MAUREEN: It's months since you've done anything so lightly.
  (*Bell rings once more.*)

BOB: That cabbie'll have his boot through the door.

MAUREEN: I'll go.

BOB: Here. Wait. Pressie. (*He takes a miniature brandy out of his pocket.*) Cheer yourself up in the train.

MAUREEN: Nice time with Del then.

BOB: Yeah.
  (*She's about to go.*)

MAUREEN: Your mum. God, I nearly forgot. Feed her, Bob.
  Nothing she can't chew. Nothing she can't swallow.

BOB: Right.

MAUREEN: Nothing she can't digest. And kiss her goodbye for me.

BOB: Haven't seen her today.

MAUREEN: She's having her lie down.

BOB: I didn't know she'd got up.

MAUREEN: Bedsores is the trade mark of your family.

BOB: Get out.
  (*MAUREEN goes. BOB opens a can. Drinks. Grins. He takes his shirt off.*)

SCENE THREE

The past. Night. Bomb-site. The young DEL comes on with an umbrella up. The umbrella has no material stretched over its spikes. This is to amuse BOB.

DEL: Bobby? That you? You here yet? (*He takes down the umbrella.*)
  No. Old prams here, lamp-shade skeletons, bits of bike, paint cans, all skinned with mud that cracks in the summer; and rotted rubber-johnnies that the niggers suck, pulling them out the mud, I've heard. Couples drive up in clapped-out Ford Anglias on Sundays after they've pulled out the fireplace, to dump the debris. White dust flying about the place, just about chokes you. All that. But no Bobby Hibbert. (*Jumps.*) What's that? (*Pause.*) Bomb-site tramp, burping off. Bet yer.

BOB: Del?

DEL: Here.

BOB: Where?

DEL: Felt myself ageing up here.

BOB: (*Runs on*) Yer dad quietened down?

DEL: It's better than valium, him thinking I'm up at the Air Cadets, practising for the Church Parade.

BOB: Ace. She's off like a baby, giving little snores, stockings rolled down; I pulled a blanket over her and got out.

DEL: You leave me with rats all about here.

BOB: Rats? Get off.

DEL: Rat shoots up me leg. Dives straight for me noodle, no mucking.

BOB: Rat wouldn't sniff that if you had a pound of Irish cheddar round it.

DEL: What you got for us tonight then?

BOB: The ol' . . . Bob Hope.

DEL: You got it?

BOB: Got it.

DEL: Phew, eh?

BOB: Here. (*Loosens his trousers.*)

DEL: Jesus.

BOB: You're telling me. (*And* BOB *brings the dope out of his underpants.*)

DEL: Dope. It looks like cow-pat.

BOB: You wanna picture of Ringo on it?

DEL: No, but –

BOB: Let's burn it. Let's have the fags.

DEL: Fags?

BOB: Tobacco. For the joint. Come on. Me mum'll –

DEL: I didn't really realize I was the monitor.

BOB: You what?

DEL: The fag monitor.

BOB: Oh Jesus, now we've come all this way.

DEL: Can't we chew it?

BOB: Chew it?

DEL: Chew it with our teeth and that.

BOB: Jesus Christ. No we can't.

DEL: I'm sorry, Bobby, I really –

BOB: Shut yer gob. (*Pause.*) What's left tonight?

DEL: Eh?

BOB: I s'pose we could –

DEL: Hey. Hey, a spot of rain! Better put up my – (*He puts up the umbrella. Smiles at* BOB. BOB *ignores it.* DEL *takes the wretched umbrella down.*)

BOB: Go down Beckenham Junction, get in the trees and chuck bricks at the Air Cadets practising for the Church Parade.

DEL: They know us from last week. No. We can –

BOB: What?

DEL: Talk.

BOB: What?

DEL: Chat and that.

BOB: We are scraping the barrel.

DEL: Chat about . . . Carol.

BOB: Carol. We've had that one.

DEL: About what she was like . . . there.

BOB: There where?

DEL: Her bush.

BOB: Her what?

DEL: Bush and that.

BOB: What am I doing – gardening?

DEL: Bob.

BOB: Oh I dunno.

DEL: I've got to tell you something . . . important.

BOB: My safety catch's off. That's one warning.

DEL: You won't say anything to anyone?

BOB: Depends on –

DEL: He's – My dad. You know, he waits up for me.

BOB: So?

DEL: Bob, he's lurking, waiting, after we've gone to the pictures with birds. He's behind the back door, and eager. Pulls me about the kitchen a bit.

BOB: My dad dragged us all about everywhere.

DEL: I know that.

BOB: They do that. Now he's gone off. Eh, you might be lucky there, eh?

DEL: And . . . he's eager for the dirty details.

BOB: What details? There aren't any details, usually.

DEL: All the details. Of what I've done.

BOB: Of what you've . . . got up?

DEL: Right.

BOB: All the dirty details he wants, I bet.

DEL: That's what I've said. Dad says: 'You been to see *Where Eagles Dare* with Rachel and Sally, mum told me.' Yeah, dad, you know I have. 'Well I'm yer dad, we're close as father and son,' he says. 'You can tell me how you got on. If you got – '

BOB: Got –

DEL: 'If yer – '

BOB: Del, Del.

DEL: 'Did yer get to Bristol? How far did yer get, eh? What you made of, soft sausage? Were you on the horn and did she – ' All the while he's pinching at my jacket. His tongue's jabbing about everywhere.

BOB: He's gobbing about the –

DEL: I could save myself a shower, couldn't I.

(BOB *laughs*.)

Don't crease up.

BOB: I'm not . . . creasing up.

DEL: Bobby.

BOB: So what d'you tell him you done?

DEL: I make up these stories. It thrills him that I'm getting on in every way.

BOB: You're not.

DEL: Couldn't you . . . you could bung me a bit of background, I thought. Give me stories that ring of the real.

BOB: Not me.

DEL: I loved that conversation we had.

BOB: What's that?

DEL: It was up here weren't it?

BOB: I can't remember everything that's ever happened to me.

DEL: Yeah, we were caught short. It opened up and came down in buckets. We crawled under the tarpaulin. Dragged it over, pinned it down all round with fire-bricks. We played pontoon with that damp pack. You were marvellous, going on.

40

BOB: Was I?

DEL: You said . . . you told me . . . that time, you had been with her in the park, behind the smelly changing-room. Go on.

BOB: I'm considering whether we can chew it or what we can do.

DEL: 'Gainst that tree. You held her. Carol. The tree dug in her. I know that tree. You were giving her a frigging. Her tights were down. She moaned all through it. You went on about it, as we played. You thought –

BOB: Shut it down five minutes can't you!

DEL: You thought, that's right, you thought . . . you could make women moan. You reckoned you were about as magnetic as the force of gravity. When you pulled her off the tree her back was bruised. After, it went the colour of blue ink. Still, wouldn't you moan if you had – (BOB *punches him*) half a branch banging into your backbone for half an hour. (*Pause.* BOB *chews the dope.*)

BOB: Umm . . . It's like chewing cement. Not bad. (*Pause.*) Hey. Do I look very . . . stoned?

DEL: Everyone knows you can't chew it!

BOB: (*Spitting it out*) Fuck it! Fuck you!

DEL: I s'pose Carol –

BOB: Why d'you keep on? Carol this, Carol that –

DEL: The old conversations.

BOB: Eh?

DEL: When it rained and we – When we were over the allotments and we – When – They're the good talks. Like the old songs. They're good songs. You wanna hear them over and over. Don't you wanna hear Chuck and Buddy and –

BOB: Tonight, tonight, right? You know what? I had it lined up. We were practically gonna carry each other back home on stretchers. I needed to be altered, tonight. My mum, she's . . . I just needed to. Smoke? I'd have sucked that tube till I honked up me lungs. The world goes gold, swims about the place, glows and that: a Beatles record. And where are we now?

DEL: Looking out over Crystal Palace.

BOB: Talking, talking. What's that?

41

DEL: Ah well.

BOB: It's you. Got no ambition for new things.

DEL: I have.

BOB: Na.

DEL: If you want, we can –

BOB: How can we? I got to get back now.

DEL: Who wants to go home?

BOB: Get back there. Go on. They'll worry.

DEL: My second wind's come through.

BOB: It's too late.

DEL: My old man. He's much worse than your mum. Oh, they'll be sitting there. They take their shoes off and rub their feet together. I wish I had your mum.

BOB: You don't know what you're saying.

DEL: Bobby.

BOB: Bye.

(BOB *runs off.* DEL *goes off.* MUM *comes forward. She's cold.*)

SCENE FOUR

MUM *in a dressing-gown over her nightie, and wearing slippers. She's waiting for* BOB. BOB *sneaks on quietly, as he tries to get past her. She turns as he comes in.*

MUM: Robert.

BOB: Mum.

MUM: Here.

BOB: What?

MUM: Here!

(*He moves towards her.*)

There you are.

BOB: Yeah. I –

MUM: You thought I was asleep.

BOB: Mum, you were.

MUM: Never mind. I'll bloody hit you.

BOB: Why?

MUM: Why d'you think?

BOB: Just bin out to see someone –

42

MUM: Who said you could?

BOB: 'Bout me homework, about that.

MUM: Where is it then?

BOB: Oh, they'll hand it in.

MUM: Where you moving off to now?

BOB: Bit of kip, I think, mum. If you don't mind.

MUM: You do look tired.

BOB: Do I?

MUM: Just come here.

BOB: Mum.

MUM: Here, I said. (*He goes to her. She examines his eyes.*) Let's have a look.

BOB: Oh get off me, mum.

MUM: That's bloodshot, that one.

BOB: It's you, poking your nail in it.

MUM: You could be so handsome if you didn't –

BOB: Mum.

MUM: You could be marvellous. Beautiful features, like I had before.

BOB: Oh you, don't tell –

MUM: Never mind that. Robert. Have you bin running across that motorway?

BOB: Eh?

MUM: When have I – I've bin at work all day. I'm too tired in the evenings to go down that freezing motorway, sweep you up.

BOB: Mum, you –

MUM: I'm out at work all day. I didn't marry your father to have to go out to work.

BOB: No.

MUM: Did I?

BOB: Any nice customers or what, today?

MUM: What?

BOB: Somebody say, anybody say anything –

MUM: What?

BOB: Nice, for a change.

MUM: Why should they?

BOB: Oh well.

MUM: Customers from the estate I've had lately.

43

BOB: Have you?

MUM: One of them paid £30 for a pair of shoes – not boots – shoes. I had a mind to say: you've got a cheek, where d'you think you got that money from?

BOB: Husband, probably.

MUM: Well, they've got a cheek.

BOB: You know, I couldn't touch those people's feet. Putting their feet into shoes and that.

MUM: Why not?

BOB: I just couldn't.

MUM: Who d'you think you are then? You think you won't work? Won't go out and do that, all day? What are you then – hereditary peer?

BOB: Mum, I respect you for it.

MUM: Thanks.

BOB: Night-night. (*He moves away.*)

MUM: Robert. Wait a minute will you.

BOB: Oh what now?

MUM: Ask us –

BOB: What?

MUM: Ask yer mum what it's like in the shop.

BOB: What?

MUM: Go on.

BOB: Mum.

MUM: Ask me.

BOB: All right. Hold on then. What's it like? What's it like . . . in the shop. (*Pause.*)

MUM: No.

BOB: What's up now?
(*She turns away.*)

BOB: Mum.

MUM: Robert it's got to stop. I mean it. You've been running across that motorway. I know you have.

BOB: X-ray eyes?

MUM: Your pants were messed.

BOB: What are you going through my pants for?

MUM: How do they get clean? What, fairies come in of a night, yank yer clothes off the bedroom floor and under a hot tap?

44

BOB: I don't think I can ever remember what that motorway looks like.

MUM: You speak and a lie pops out. It's automatic with you. Like a slot-machine. You can't help yourself.

BOB: Oh Jesus.

MUM: Why don't I spoil myself? Why don't I go mad and ruin myself with everything I want? Why don't I – What have you done – When have you lifted a finger for me? When have you then? When? When?

(Pause.)

BOB: Oh God.

MUM: Eh?

BOB: My eye feels a bit bloodshot.

MUM: Does it?

BOB: So I'm off up, I think; take the strain off it in this light.

MUM: Shut that top window.

BOB: What?

MUM: Get up on the hall chair and pull that window to. Catch a draught and you'll wake up moaning in the morning with a stiff –

BOB: Stiff what?

MUM: Well.

(They laugh.)

You.

(He kisses her.)

BOB: Night-night.

MUM: God bless.

BOB: God bless.

(He goes. She unties her long grey hair, which is knotted at the back of her neck, and lets it fall.)

MUM: Both my babies, safe in bed. I can lock the back door now. Then I'll put my feet up for a – if I'm not too tired to move them. Oh, I'd better put the tea things away before I – for the morning. That Julie never lifts a finger. Not that I want her to. Not that she does anything voluntarily. Not that he does, ever. Oh no, not him. It's only me who does anything here. I'd better –

(She dozes off.)

45

Morning. The present. Lights up bright. DEL *on stage.* BOB *there too.*
DEL: Woke up early. Fine morning. Shaved. Cut myself. Ran out
of the house I share with three other teachers, cotton wool
hanging off my cheek. Bob's wife Maureen had rung me the
week before. She was worried. He was . . . No. I did want to
see him. (*Pause.*) It had been a long time. I had vowed never
to . . . Still, it was exciting. Didn't know what to . . . (*Pause.
Then very fast.*) Came down through South London it's the
same through New Cross and that, 47 bus, before I go to
sleep like to drift back, nearly every night now I'm back . . .
there. (*Slight pause.*) As the lights came up in the Orpington
Odeon. Our house seemed to have. As the lights came up in
the Orpington Odeon, yellow light on young faces round
you, silence in the cinema a moment, then fiercely
determined bang bang bang seats snapping back people
stirring. I want to go for, say there were . . . thick walls so
our house seemed sound-proofed, deep-bricked, cut-out
almost, by sheer coldness of attitude, from the rest of the
road, and all the other roads like it, that dribbled like
tributaries towards the Thames eight miles away. You took
your hand from between her legs. No; that's invented, talked
of, yearned for. Warm, you took your hand from between
your legs. Better. With Bob, up the slope cinema aisle jeeze
blimey me leg's gone to sleep. Shabby you are, skin feeling
grey after brightness what's on next week where are we going
tonight then? Up the . . . late evening at the dinner table you
spread out your correspondence course, them gin and sofa
slumped you thought how thick the walls seemed. Not that
really, only that outside there was no sound, no activity,
nothing. You felt pressed under water, TV periscope letting
in grey light from out there. Back row black boots on saw
Help! nine times YELLS John! John! We love you true! We
do. (*Pause.*) Take those disgusting boots off: telly's on: quiet,
quiet, quiet! Two hundred nicker carpet sacred strip stripey
number yellow stripey wallpaper. Older, in Levis, I said to
dad: this room, I mean, I could be sitting in a Bridget Riley

painting. I mean. He slapped me. No: I swore at him. Home from work his arm banging fury *Readers' Digest* flying off the mantelpiece, family scattering like frightened fowl – woman pick them up! Ah work, work, the working life, something they did to him made him squeeze me between the bars, and out in the air, educated, a paste of learning thinly spread over me to make me tasty for genteel employers. Trapped in trains the men'd come home while down by the railway us stripped-down scornful scorching on the railway bank on flattened thistles semi-erect proud something has to be sorted out . . .

BOB: Later, Later.

DEL: Bob.

BOB: Del. Have a drink. Come on.

DEL: Sure?

BOB: I can't really natter while a man's suffering, can I? (*He tosses the beer-can over.*)

DEL: How are you affording all this refreshment?

BOB: What? You gone soft or something since I seen you?

DEL: Only in the belly.

BOB: Ha. I borrowed from everyone I know. Fuck 'em, I say. It's you. Oldest friend, eh?
(DEL *drinks.*)
What an evening.

DEL: Eh?

BOB: You know, I tell you; tonight, right, I could get excited by the stars. Leaves, bits of fence: little things could get to me.

DEL: Not like you.

BOB: Exactly. Now, either – (*He drinks.*) This is pretty good.

DEL: Bobby. You're making me crack me head against a wall. There's something I've come to clear up.

BOB: In good time. You're looking a bit stiff, a bit dead. Let yourself go. Come on. Or I'll have to bash you. (*And throws beer over* DEL.) Cool down.

DEL: Oh Jesus.
(BOB *laughs.*)
Don't bully me about.

BOB: I will. Me wife's away.

DEL: So?

47

BOB: Well. Let us breathe a bit. Let me open my chest. I tell you, when she went I stripped right down, naked. I walked about the house. Felt the old place between my toes again. You got a girlfriend?

DEL: Yeah.

BOB: You'll know the relief I'm on about. You're not being watched, when they go. The incredible pleasure of not being seen all the time, eh? (*Pause.*) Now, my friend. Either we fester here like a couple of old grandads –

DEL: Or –

BOB: Or . . . we break out. Tonight.

DEL: Break out where?

BOB: Get out. Over the old places.

DEL: You know them; better than your own dick you know them.

BOB: Much better. Every let-down tyre: I'll tell you when, where and how much. All of us unemployed do plenty of tramping about.

DEL: Why don't you tell me how long it's been now.

BOB: Since I lifted a finger?

DEL: How long? Can you remember?

BOB: You don't wanna get into all that.

DEL: I do, very much.

BOB: All right. After the garage gave me the push . . . You know about that.

DEL: Yes.

BOB: Well, I was a van driver. Then a packer, porter, scenery-shifter, caretaker; barrow-boy – no, they went bust. That was two years back. No: more, now. I'm not counting. Maureen's counting. Constantly.

DEL: Maybe you must try to find –

BOB: What?

DEL: I only thought you must –

BOB: 'Course. I must. I must, eh? (*Pause.*) Del. I'll be honest. You'll like that. Might as well be.

DEL: Go on.

BOB: You tell me why I should wanna work now? How many mornings are my peepers open before eleven? Who's telling me where to stand? Or what time to eat my dinner? Or how many chews to take?

DEL: Discouragement's about the worst thing, isn't it?

BOB: You say so. I'm too far gone for any serious sweating. I mean it.

DEL: You do seem –

BOB: I seem. Do I seem?

DEL: Bob . . .

BOB: Del. You. You par for the course are you then? Teaching. Nice people to natter to in the staff room?

DEL: The kids are . . . lively.

BOB: Not like us, I bet. Pulling chunks out the blackboard; chunks out the teachers.

DEL: They're exactly like that. I'm interested in you, and work, all that, for their future. Now tell me, is it you can't find work – I don't know this area now – or –

BOB: Doctor Del.

DEL: Get back in the habit, Bobby.

BOB: No!

DEL: You've got to.

BOB: Not now. (*Pause.*) Not a scrubber, me. I'm not anybody's. No. I've got no job. I'm independent. I fear no one. Right?

DEL: You bet. But –

BOB: No, I said. I won't be a shit-sculptor no more. I'm putting on airs now. Let someone else suck shit. Them blacks.

DEL: Oh Jesus.

BOB: Let them. If they can't get no one else to do it. (*Pause.*)

DEL: This isn't going to be such a big laugh.

BOB: Let anyone.

DEL: Bobby.

BOB: Can't understand how you can have yer moral orgasm with me. After what you've done to a man. A brown man, he was, even in the dark.

DEL: Yes. All right.

BOB: How can you? Don't you remember?

DEL: Yes.

BOB: Eh?

DEL: Yes.

49

BOB: Do you?

DEL: Most days, I do.

BOB: Well, good. Good.

DEL: Nothing'll be resolved tonight. I'll get on the train, I think.
(*Pause.*) The booze.

BOB: What?

DEL: Hope it didn't cost yer.

BOB: No. It didn't cost me, really.
(DEL *puts his hand out to shake with* BOB.)

DEL: Bye then.
(MUM *has entered in her dressing-gown. She has become old.*)

BOB: Mum.

MUM: Robert.

BOB: You have your lie down?

DEL: (*Whispers to* BOB) That's your mum . . . isn't it?

BOB: It's Anna Neagle.

DEL: Mrs Hibbert, hallo.

BOB: Go back to bed, mum. Got something to read? Can't you sleep
now?
(*She shakes her head.*)
Is it them people making a noise outside the Indian takeaway?
I'll bloody –

DEL: Mrs Hibbert. Can't you get off to sleep?

BOB: No. She's in pain.

DEL: Can I ask . . . what sort of pain is it?

BOB: Mum. Derek wants to know which pain is it tonight.

MUM: The same pain. In the same place.

BOB: (*To* DEL) That put you in the picture?

DEL: What does she do now, your mum?

BOB: What does she do? Hasn't she done enough? (*To* MUM.) Is it
your tummy or your head? (*To* DEL.) She gets vibrations in
her stomach. (MUM *turns away. To* DEL.) Feel queer yourself?

DEL: I –

BOB: It's only mum. You know mum. She's not gone stupid.

DEL: 'Course not.

BOB: Just sick of things.

DEL: Yes.

BOB: Makes you wanna live. Live. Makes me. Eh? Cut out. And

live it up.

DEL: Is your sister here?

BOB: Fled. Emigrated. South Africa. Mum took it bad. (*To* MUM.) Mum. Mum.

MUM: Oh Robert, what is it now?

BOB: Oh come on, say how's yer arm, to silly old Derek. Remember him? Little bugger'd have half-crowns out yer purse before you could say a prayer.

MUM: Don't be daft. I remember you, Derek. I see yer mum round the corner. She's on her own now.

DEL: Yes, she is.

BOB: (*To* MUM) He's a teacher now.

MUM: Are you, duck?

BOB: Up London.

MUM: Glad you're earning your keep then. Good boy. That's marvellous.

BOB: Come on mum. Back to bye-byes.

DEL: Night-night, Mrs Hibbert.

(BOB *takes her off.* DEL *cracks another can.* BOB *returns.*)

BOB: Oh. Thought you'd be well on the bus by now.

DEL: Near thing.

BOB: Yeah. So you're over yer little rush.

DEL: If you shut up I will be.

BOB: Let's go then.

DEL: Okay.

BOB: I tell you. With you tonight . . . all that'll seem fresh again. You can do that to me, you little jerk.

DEL: Can I?

BOB: What's matter?

DEL: No, it's nothing.

BOB: No, there is. Oh. She puts it on. She does now. Had enough of working. Shop gave her the shove.

DEL: Why?

BOB: And the routine wore her through . . . in places. Here – (*Gives him a couple of cans and puts some in his own pockets.*) Great chance tonight eh?

DEL: What for, old son?

BOB: Rise above things.

DEL: Bleedin' angel you now, eh?

BOB: Yeah.

DEL: We'll see.

BOB: And we will. (*Pause.*) Come on out.

DEL: It's been a while.

BOB: It has.

SCENE SIX

The past. BOB *combing his hair.* DEL *comes on behind him.*

DEL: Bob.

BOB: Here. I'm in here. Come through.

DEL: Right.

BOB: Hiya.

DEL: We out tonight? (*Pause.*) Are we?

BOB: 'Course we are.

DEL: Thought we might not be.

BOB: 'Course we're out.

DEL: That's okay.

BOB: Outta my light.

DEL: It's uncanny.

BOB: Del, listen.

DEL: No, it is.

BOB: Is it?

DEL: You're turning into Cliff Richard, gradually.

BOB: Keith Richard, you mean; Keith.

DEL: Na. It's his brother I see in you.

BOB: Hank Marvin? Na. Have I got the goggles?

DEL: No, but your head's the right shape.

BOB: You shouldn't have let me down on my big day. I'm waiting
    for you by the building-site off Pope Road, standing about
    like a pratt.

DEL: Got on the 94 at the traffic-lights. Had this ton of
    homework.

BOB: You weren't where I expected.

DEL: Tell you, I'm at the kitchen table with two set squares when
    dad comes in from work. He smells of the train. He has these

52

two whiskies and mum makes a run for it out the front door.
He smells of whisky.

BOB: Del. Guess what, Del.

DEL: I can practically smell him from the next room. I get up
slowly. I can hear him banging the books down in there.
Then I'm out through the French windows.

BOB: Del.

DEL: So here I am.

BOB: Go on, guess it man!

DEL: Guess what?

BOB: Na. Okay. Don't bother to unlock your brain-box. I won't
tell you. (*Pause.*) Jesus, Del, can I get me hair right. (*He
continues combing.*)

DEL: Give it another hour.

BOB: Look at these tufts going up at the back, sprouting out like a
bog brush.

DEL: Come on then.

BOB: What?

DEL: Hold still a minute. (*Holds* BOB's *head and brushes his hair
down by spitting into his hand and smoothing it across.*) Hold
still! (*Pause.*) She wants you, she says.

BOB: When?

DEL: Now. She's down there with your sister.

BOB: I haven't hardly got into me Sta-Prest.

DEL: Don't prance about!

BOB: It's gone again!

DEL: All over. (*Holds* BOB's *head and brushes down the naughty tufts
once more.*)

BOB: Gotta look a bit casual. Tonight's a big one.

DEL: Janet?

BOB: Na. Look. I'm leaving. D'you know that? No, well, I'm
out, at last.

DEL: Are you?

BOB: Aren't you?

DEL: No.

BOB: Well.

DEL: What are you going to be?

BOB: Motor mechanic. Garage taking me on. Looking forward to it. Proper work.

DEL: Yeah.

BOB: £8 a week. That's basic.

DEL: It is.

BOB: A trade, I'll have. Be able to build dragsters from scratch. Racing cars. Anything. Your dad.

DEL: What?

BOB: The pervert. He wants you to be an architect or violinist. Tough shit, schoolboy.

DEL: Doesn't matter what he wants.

BOB: Doesn't it?

DEL: No.

BOB: Just that you haven't got –

DEL: What?

BOB: Will of your own.

DEL: Reckon?

BOB: My old lady. The other week she hauls me into her bedroom. Begs me to stay on at school. I tell her it's too late. Education's passed me by. She seems to agree with that. Because she had to.

DEL: They expect a lot from me, my mum and dad. Not just –

MUM: (*Off*) Robert!

BOB: Not just?

DEL: She's calling. You'd better go.

MUM: Robert! Here!

DEL: Tell you, it's important for once. Go down to her.

BOB: Hang on. (*Pause*.) Not just? What am I? Not just. Just a shit-shoveller you mean: a turd-turner. What are you then?

DEL: Didn't mean that.

BOB: Didn't you?

DEL: I mean –

BOB: Next week, right, even then, next Saturday at nine, I'll be in scenes you'll beg me to take you into. In two years . . . you'll still be in uniform! I'll have wardrobes of gear. I'll have to borrow your cupboard. Won't be no room here! Wanna borrow a tenner? Wanna see what a tenner looks like? (*Pause*.)

DEL: Come on down. She'll do her nut.

BOB: Creep show.

DEL: Comb your hair –

BOB: What?

DEL: Put your head up your arse.

> (*They go off.*
> JULIA, *Bob's sister, is lying back, a slice of cucumber over each eye, a soft drink in one hand. She is wearing a long, frilly petticoat.*)

JULIA: . . . I would.

MUM: (*Off*) Yes.

JULIA: So. What did you say?

MUM: I said, I said to her: if I can't have one Saturday afternoon off to go and see a matinée at the Festival Hall with my daughter once in a blue moon that is; if I can't do that after all these years of –

JULIA: Loyal service to them.

MUM: I have been loyal. That's the thing. Then bugger them – I'll walk right out.

JULIA: I'd put out the flags if you did.

MUM: They keep saying the firm's like a big family. But you always feel like you're a distant relative or something.

JULIA: You won't walk out.

MUM: I could do anything when they treat you like that.

JULIA: You won't.

MUM: Don't say that.

JULIA: They've got you by the tits.

MUM: And they –

JULIA: Mum, can't you hurry up with that dress?

MUM: What?

JULIA: Come on! Jesus!

MUM: You wait a minute! I'll come out there and – Don't you want it ironed properly?

JULIA: Ironed? You've gone through it. You're ironing the carpet.

MUM: Don't be stupid.

> (BOB *and* DEL *appear.*)

JULIA: Mum, that's it then, I'm –

MUM: What? What? I can't hear you properly.

55

JULIA: Oh . . . chuck it in the – how can I wear that now? Jesus!

MUM: Julia, it's all right. (*Lower voice.*) God's honour, it's all right.

    (BOB *bends over and pokes his bum towards* JULIA.)

JULIA: (*Mutters*) 'Course it's bloody burning, what's that smell –

BOB: I let one off!

JULIA: (*Plucking away her pieces of cucumber*) You bastard!

DEL: Watch out Bobby!

    (*She swipes at him.*)

JULIA: Great baboon!

MUM: What's happening in there?

BOB: (*To* MUM) What?

MUM: Have I got to come in?

JULIA: (*To* BOB) Don't you come near me, wanker! I'll bloody hit you.

MUM: Don't make me come in!

BOB: Where's that cucumber, I'll show you how to use it.

JULIA: Mum! Quick!

    (MUM *runs in.*)

MUM: What are you doing with her?

BOB: Oh shut up!

JULIA: It's always him!

MUM: Keep out of her way – you animal!

JULIA: Mum, mum, where's my dress?

MUM: Oh give me five minutes to myself will you Julia!

JULIA: I want to look at my dress!

BOB: Jesus Christ! (*He runs off.*)

MUM: Don't touch that!

JULIA: Oh leave it!

DEL: Bobby.

    (BOB *returns with the dress.*)

BOB: Here's the rotten thing. I'll fucking –

JULIA: Don't touch that!

DEL: Bobby.

MUM: Robert.

BOB: Here Del, I reckon I'll wear it on me nodder.

MUM: (*Snatching it*) Robert give it to your sister.

    (*Gives it to* JULIA.)

56

Here you are, now –
(JULIA *throws it down*.)
Julia!
JULIA: It's not fit – How can I wear it? Everyone's wiped the kitchen floor with it. Like a hankie he's snotted into.
BOB: Weeping Jesus!
(*Pause*.)
MUM: Bobby go out somewhere.
BOB: I might get killed on the motorway.
MUM: Out of my sight!
BOB: (*Angry*) No, no, why should I? Why d'you treat her like this?
MUM: What? Like what?
BOB: Why mum?
MUM: I don't know what –
JULIA: Don't talk to the useless wanker they've chucked out of school. He can't even –
BOB: (*To* MUM) Treating her like . . . royalty. Practically –
MUM: If you'd like to know . . . she is royalty to me.
JULIA: I am fucking royalty to her.
BOB: For Christ's sake!
MUM: Robert what makes you think – do you really think – I want her to learn to be a skivvy like I am? Like I've been? Always will be? A house-cleaner and that. Putting shoes on people's feet like I – No! Not her. Not my daughter.
JULIA: Not me!
MUM: And I don't want her to be treated by you like – (*Pause*.) Oh Jesus.
DEL: Mrs Hibbert.
MUM: I've given myself a bloody great headache listening to this face-ache.
JULIA: (*Going*) I'll have to wear what I had on last week, and risk it! (*She goes off*.)
BOB: (*To* DEL, *indicating that they might sneak off out of it*.) Del, I reckon –
MUM: Where you two think you're going?
BOB: Out. You just said –
MUM: You hang on here five minutes now.

57

BOB: What for?

MUM: You can't wait for nothing can you. (*Pause.*) Something I've ordered has arrived for you.

BOB: What has?

MUM: My head's spinning.

BOB: Mum what's arrived?

MUM: What do you deserve anyway? (*To* DEL) Derek. You go and get it from the airing cupboard. Bring everything.

DEL: Right Mrs Hibbert.

MUM: Good boy.

(*He goes off.*)

BOB: What is it?

MUM: You'll see it if you stand still a minute.

BOB: This isn't like you, mum.

MUM: Shut your mouth!

(DEL *comes on with an electric guitar, a small amp and an instruction manual.*)

DEL: Here you are.

BOB: What's that, mum?

MUM: (*To* DEL) Isn't he a nit at times? Most of the time, I should say.

BOB: Electric guitar.

DEL: Ten points.

BOB: Where d'you knock it off from, mum.

MUM: Can't you ever be nice?

DEL: She saved up.

BOB: Oh mum.

DEL: Weeks and weeks it took her.

MUM: It did.

BOB: Can I – (*He goes to take it.*)

MUM: Get off it will you Robert!

BOB: I thought –

MUM: Who said you could – Don't touch that 'til I've said – You listen: learn to play that blasted thing! I mean it. Here's a book with charts and codes. You read it and –

BOB: All right, mum.

MUM: Please Robert, no mucking about in your usual way.

BOB: Don't go on.

58

MUM: Get down the shed away from everyone and practise. (*To* DEL) Give him a chance, I thought. He's useless at school.

BOB: Mum.

MUM: You are. I've known it months.

BOB: (*To* DEL) I've known it years.

MUM: Thanks for letting me know. (*To* DEL) I had a letter from Mr Haggard, your headmaster. He won't have Robert back at school. I begged him to have him next year.

BOB: I'll be a motor mechanic.

MUM: You?

BOB: Yes I will.

MUM: You couldn't mechanic a shoe-box. Now get off.

BOB: Can I –

MUM: Take it. Take it. (*Pause.*) Oh good luck to yer.
(*He kisses her. He goes.*)

DEL: I didn't know he was musical.

MUM: He's a boy. His dad's gone. Nobody knows where. I wish I could give him the attention your dad gives you.

DEL: Yes.

MUM: And still Robert's –

DEL: Mrs Hibbert, my tea's on the – I think I better go.

MUM: All right. Now quickly tell me what your mum's going to do with you.

DEL: Well they . . . I don't really know.

MUM: You're staying at school though?

DEL: Ol' Haggard says so. And they're forcing me to; yes.

MUM: I can't force mine. You with your brains and background. You'll do marvellous. Know it too.

DEL: Do I?

MUM: I'd be more surprised if mine did anything. (*Pause.*) Now. What's all this I've heard about –

DEL: What, Mrs Hibbert?

MUM: Him getting tattooed.

DEL: I don't know what you mean.

MUM: What d'you think of me? Have I got omelette in my head, eh? Haven't I got ears that pick things up now and again?

DEL: Leave it out, Mrs Hibbert!

MUM: Well, Derek, just you tell me –

59

DEL: Oh I don't know. I've got to go.

MUM: Hang on. Half a minute.

DEL: You see, well, he wants this 'W' tattooed on each cheek –

MUM: His face?

DEL: Of his bum, Mrs Hibbert. Of his arse, and that.

MUM: What the bloody hell for?

DEL: So that when he bends over it spells 'wow'.
(*Pause.*)

MUM: Oh where will it all lead?

DEL: They're tattooed, all the boys. Their girlfriends don't sleep with them – they read them!

MUM: Show me yours.

DEL: I'm not. And they think I'm soft.

MUM: Where will it get him eventually?

DEL: I don't think it counts as an O level. It might get him a CSE.

MUM: Will he . . . is he good enough to play for the Palace?

DEL: I said to him: you go up the Millwall – make 'em give you a trial.

MUM: What did they say?

DEL: Did he go? I reckon he might be good at blow-football. If he practised.

MUM: That's what you think of my son, is it?

DEL: Oh, don't ask me.

MUM: No. (*She stares at him.*) He's got that banjo now. Keep him quiet five minutes. These days could lead to anything.

DEL: Yeah. Could.

MUM: Can't it? Don't want him to –

DEL: Sit down Mrs Hibbert, if you've got a bad head.

MUM: Just –

DEL: I'll get you a chair.

MUM: Oh, I don't know what to do with him. (*Pause.*) Don't tell me to sit down.

DEL: You should.

MUM: How can I? I've got to get their dinner on yet.

DEL: Send the lazy buggers up the chippie.

MUM: They can't eat all that grease. Derek, you go home, go on, you better, if your poor mum's got yours on.

DEL: All right. Bye, Mrs Hibbert.

MUM: Derek. (*Pause.*) Oh I don't know. Go on.
DEL: He'll be . . . great.
MUM: Will he? (*Pause.*) I don't know why I worry. I really don't.
DEL: No.

> (*He goes.* MUM *stands there. Long fade.*
> *In the fade we hear the sound of a novice twanging an electric*
> *guitar.*
> *Fade to blackout.*)

SCENE SEVEN

The present. The bomb-site. Night. Stars in the sky. DEL *behind* BOB,
following him up over the debris.

BOB: Come on.
DEL: Bobby.
BOB: Up here.
DEL: Bob.
BOB: What's up?
DEL: I'm tired.
BOB: Come on.
DEL: Where are we going anyway?
BOB: Just follow me up.
DEL: Where?
BOB: Top of the world. (*Pause.*) What a night it is. Look at the
    sky. Look.
DEL: What?
BOB: Don't you remember this place?
DEL: Should I?
BOB: We'd come here.
DEL: Jesus. Yes. High up.
BOB: Right.
DEL: I remember it now.
BOB: Look out over London.

> (*They look.* BOB *pulls out a bottle.*)

    Here. Warm up. Enjoy your life.
DEL: Ta.

61

BOB: So . . . what's it like, seeing it again?

DEL: Well . . . coming up, I thought: I must be a bit of a genius. I've done it. What I wanted. I'm well out.

BOB: That what you think?

DEL: Of course. This is the edge, isn't it? On the outskirts, we are now. And I'll always think of it that way.

BOB: This was our patch.

DEL: Yes.

BOB: We knew it.

DEL: Every inch.

BOB: Now it's being taken over.

DEL: Is it?

BOB: Oh yeah. There are all sorts, moving over it. People behave as if they own it. The wrong people, as if they belong here. They don't know who we are. They don't have any respect for us. They make a noise. Some of them have got money. We don't seem to have any . . . clout. You know.

DEL: What?

BOB: I still come up here.

DEL: When?

BOB: Of an afternoon. Mornings, you're yelling at kids to quieten down. I'm turning over the garden again. Banging up a kitchen shelf; putting down a bet. Or I'm in line, up the dole. Then I get out, of an afternoon.

DEL: Haven't you got anything better to do?

BOB: Out in the air. I like to get out the house.

DEL: What d'you do?

BOB: Do?

DEL: Yes, d'you –

BOB: Sit down. Walk about.

DEL: In the winter?

BOB: I don't care about that. Come up here anytime.

DEL: Alone?

BOB: What are you on about? I think of you.

DEL: Why?

BOB: Whopping sense into idiots, reading yer paper in the staff room. You have long holidays and that, why don't we get

together more? We could go to matches. Get out to the
pictures. Anything.

DEL: You know . . . There are . . . black children, in my class at
school. Children of all colours. We learn about their
cultures. The rest of the world can't be excluded. The rest of
the world interests us.
(*Pause.*)

BOB: Up here . . .

DEL: What?

BOB: You know why I like it? (BOB *takes off his jacket and rolls up
his shirt sleeves*.) I feel my strength coming back. My blood
seems stirred up. It's not much of an oasis.

DEL: This place, no.

BOB: Filthy tip. You can't see the sea. There's no palm trees. But
I'm up here more and more. Get my energy up. Recharge
myself. Then I go down to meet the lads, of an evening.

DEL: D'you think . . . is something happening to you?

BOB: Hey.

DEL: Tell me, right, give me some idea if something's –

BOB: Am I getting headaches you mean?

DEL: I want you to tell me if you're, well, changing in any way. If
you feel different, or worse now, say; if what's happened
over the last two years feels like –

BOB: Feels like –

DEL: Sickness.

BOB: Ah.

DEL: That might be a way of putting it; of describing something
you can't stop, for example, that's kind of crawled over you.

BOB: You've got the whine off to a T.

DEL: Eh?

BOB: Maureen.

DEL: They aren't meant badly, these questions, friend.

BOB: Oh. Then I'm fine, fine. This country, if anything, that's
the ill one; not me. I'll do something one day. (*Slight pause.*)
All right. You want to know.

DEL: Go on.

BOB: There's an organization. I belong to it. It's not . . . the
Labour Party.

63

DEL: You don't really have the right class background do you?

BOB: Shut up. It's . . . we're strong men, together. Men worn down by waiting. Abused men. Men with no work. Our parents made redundant. Now us. No joke. Wandering round the place, like people stranded on holiday. We've talked. We agree on plenty of things. Now we've started something serious. We've joined with other groups. We're nothing to do with soft politics. No pussyfooting, with this group. Things will be changed.

DEL: This fascist organization.

BOB: Wait a minute, Del.

DEL: Eh?

(BOB *digs in the earth with his hands*.)

BOB: Just give it a wait five minutes, all right?

DEL: Are you planting seeds?

BOB: I told you. Hang on. (*Pause*.) There's something in here. Want to show you.

DEL: What is it?

(BOB *pulls a filthy Indian passport out of the ground*.)

BOB: Well now.

DEL: Bobby.

BOB: Here we are.

DEL: Eh?

BOB: Look.

(DEL *looks*.)

We beat this man.

DEL: All right.

BOB: There's his brown mug.

DEL: Yes.

BOB: Didn't we give him a bang that night, eh? You and me. He could easily have copped it, that night.

DEL: He didn't. He's still walking about.

BOB: But with a limp, I bet.

DEL: Years ago, all that.

BOB: Still stings.

DEL: We didn't think then. It was only feeling we wanted. We had to be burned . . . to feel anything.

BOB: So?

64

DEL: Just tell me. Where the hell d'you think you got this?
BOB: Went back for it.
DEL: That night?
BOB: Mum was asleep. You were. I came out.
DEL: Why, for Christ's sake?
BOB: Little souvenir, I thought.
DEL: No. It didn't happen.
BOB: This proves something.
DEL: You don't . . . yap about it. You don't go mouthing off about it do you?
BOB: Well.
DEL: Jesus you do.
BOB: I didn't say so.
DEL: Tell me, Bobby.
BOB: People are proud of me. Solid English people are behind me. Ordinary people give little cheers.
DEL: I can imagine.
BOB: You're shook, little one.
DEL: Up yours.
BOB: Strong movement, we are. Powerful activity. I like that. Cut through the muck. Things get done. It's not like you're doing everything under a pile of blankets.
DEL: You want blood. You think it's the same as change.
BOB: We know what we're up to. We're getting response.
DEL: You know, what we did, years ago, you can't elevate it now. It wasn't meant, in that way. It happened . . . as things happen. Thrust out of muddle. Random combinations, sparking off, like billiard balls shooting about. Not meant. We wanted sensation. I did. We were kids. Children who stomped on ants and banged down knives between our fingers. Only –
BOB: We were cleaning something up. I understand that now.
DEL: Mad misconceived children.
BOB: I know what people want. I can feel their feelings. I walk round the estates. I hear everything here.
DEL: Well I know what they need. (*Pause.*) Give us that.
BOB: Eh?
DEL: Give me that, Bob. Hand me that muck. Hand it to me. (*Pause.*)

BOB: I might need to be reminded of something.

DEL: Oh Jesus. (*Pause.*) My career.

BOB: Ah. Now you're talking.

DEL: All right, all right. It's the thing – the only thing, which gives me pleasure. I love learning . . . and teaching. And it is the one thing: reason's the one thing that can cut through the muck. People with minds, lighting up small areas. People with proper minds. We're nothing otherwise. Nothing, if we can't see clearly what's happening; what's being done. (*Pause.*) You know you can smash me.

BOB: Don't snivel all over the place.

DEL: Bob.

BOB: It makes me feel ill.

DEL: Give me that.

BOB: And you'll get on your bike back to your Islington.

DEL: No.

BOB: What? You can't wait.

DEL: I came to have a time, right? It's good to be with you.
(BOB *hands* DEL *the passport.*)
Thanks.

BOB: What does it mean? It's nothing to me. It's actions that add up.
(*Pause.*)

DEL: You must be half froze. Put that jacket back on.

BOB: Bit of cold doesn't bother me.

DEL: I'm going to burn this. Then we'll get back. We can talk there.

BOB: If you want.

DEL: Come on Bobby.

BOB: You don't understand what it's like.

DEL: Will you follow me down?

BOB: Okay.

DEL: Right.
(DEL *sets fire to the passport. They go off with it blazing.*)

The past. Outside the disco. Night BOB *on stage.* DEL *comes out. The Moody Blues' 'Knights in White Satin' in the background.*

DEL: For Christ's sake.

BOB: What?

DEL: There you are.

BOB: So?

DEL: That disco's shagged me. My clothes are all stuck to me. It's like wearing water. I wish we'd brought out some of your mum's talc to put on.

BOB: Been dancing then?

DEL: Na, trying to get to the bar. Looked for you. D'you wanna fag?

BOB: Ta. Yeah.
    (*They light up.*)

DEL: What are you doing now then?

BOB: I'm out here.

DEL: Why? Oh come back in.

BOB: What for?

DEL: They're playing the record. He read out the request for you. The disc jockey. Snivellin' Steven or whatever his name is.

BOB: Our names?

DEL: You and Maureen. Yeah.

BOB: You didn't tell me you were gonna set that up you cheeky bugger.

DEL: They're playing 'Knights in White Satin'. The one you like. She's thrilled.

BOB: 'Course she is.

DEL: You're missing it. They've turned the lights down and everyone's swaying to the music. People are smooching. Joints are going round. It's lovely. Maureen's waiting on her own. You can't leave her there now. Only the second time you're out together. She still gets you going doesn't she?

BOB: Mind yer own, will you?

DEL: I've just had a little talk with her and she wants to come and watch you play on Sunday morning against the Post Office Eleven. She says she'll come.

67

BOB: You invited her over the Brickfield to watch me play against the Post Office?

DEL: Listen.

BOB: She knows I turn out for the Gas Board team?

DEL: No, Christ, wait a minute. She know you –

BOB: What? What?

DEL: All about how you nearly played for the Palace. How you're naturally left-footed and that. How they compared you to John White.

BOB: How does she know all this then?

DEL: I told her.

BOB: What are you, my manager? You'll be wanting commission. I don't believe it.

DEL: Come on. Come in. Come on, Bob.

BOB: No. She's got to understand I get moody and that.

DEL: Hey, I've got a bit moody, you know. We had some times, at school.

BOB: Didn't we.

DEL: That time we –

BOB: Yeah. Forget it. What'll we do tonight?

DEL: What?

BOB: It's early. Don't you fancy a bit of activity tonight?

DEL: Yeah. If you want.

BOB: Celebrate.

DEL: I'm out, if you are.

BOB: You don't wanna go back in there?

DEL: No.

BOB: It's a waste. It's not just any night tonight. That's what I was thinking. Look. See this. Look. (BOB *spins round on the spot.*) Free movement.

DEL: What?

BOB: You know, I got nothing holding me. No teachers now, no women, parents, nothing. I'm away. I tell you, Del, it's all waiting for a boy like me. Cars, clothes, crumpet.

DEL: If you work hard.

BOB: That's right. And it feels good, good to think about money in your pocket.

DEL: Yeah, it must.

BOB: Right. Tonight we'll be active. Up the motorway if you like.

DEL: We haven't run across that one for ages.

BOB: There you are then. We'll do that run one last time before I go on to higher things.

DEL: What better things have I got to go on to?

BOB: You? Here. You'd better guzzle this then. (*Gives him a small bottle of whisky.*) Don't worry. Maybe a bit of hyperactivity tonight.

DEL: The boot goes in.

BOB: You.

DEL: What?

BOB: Talking like that.

DEL: (*Hands back bottle*) I'm fortified.

BOB: You must be.

DEL: I thought we'd be hanging round Maureen all night.

BOB: Not now.

DEL: Right.

BOB: Tell you, Del, tell you, there's hardly enough night for all I want to get up to.

DEL: Let's shift then.

BOB: Right.

(*They run off.*

MUM *comes on in her nightie and slippers. She has an overcoat wrapped around her.*)

MUM: (*Calling*) Robert! Robert! I'm going to lock the back door now. Here's the key. You in that shed? There's no lights on. He's not in there in the dark? Can't hear him twanging that banjo. Robert! I bet I know . . . he's gone over Mrs Weaver's garden, out her front gate. Bastard. If he's sold that thing straight away I'll have his guts for garters. I'll have those golf-clubs down and give him a hiding. Oh God, this grass is wet. My feet are frozen. My slippers are soaked through. They'll be in trouble with the police. Robert!

(*She goes off.*)

The present. Late at night. Back at the house after their look around the old places.

BOB: Jesus, that was a jaunt, eh?

DEL: What a kid you still are.

BOB: I enjoy myself.

DEL: You wouldn't rather be out with your friends tonight?

BOB: Last night we were out.

DEL: Ah.

BOB: Drink to bring you down?

DEL: I'm okay for the moment.

BOB: Are you? I'm having one. I'm having ten. I need it.

DEL: Have ten.

BOB: I will, I think. (*He opens a can.*) Game of cards?

DEL: No.

BOB: What's matter?

DEL: The toe of me shoe's practically scuffed off.

BOB: You were in them shoes when I knew you. I s'pose you buy books and video equipment now.

DEL: It's not that. You should have mentioned on the phone we were hiking up the Eiger.

BOB: Don't the old places mean anything to you?

DEL: Well, they –

BOB: Don't they?

DEL: Bob I got other things to think about and go on to. Believe me, there's more . . . attractive places.

BOB: (*Holding up a beer*) Sure you won't?

DEL: I think I'll get my head down.

BOB: Already?

DEL: It'll amaze you, but I'm knackered.

BOB: No, not yet.

DEL: Tomorrow we'll –

BOB: No. Now! She's hardly out the house, these days. You don't understand what a treat it is. Come on. D'you wanna hear some sounds?

DEL: Bobby, come on.

BOB: You wanna dance? Dance with me. Come on. Let's do the

Hokey-Cokey! (*He sings some of the 'Hokey-Cokey'.* MUM
comes on in her perennial dressing-gown.)

MUM: What's this row now?

BOB: Mum we're only up chatting.

MUM: Funny chatting.

DEL: Sorry Mrs Hibbert.

BOB: (*Mimicking* DEL) Sorry Mrs Hibbert.

MUM: (*To* DEL) Isn't he still a boy?

DEL: He's a bit of a kid, yes.

BOB: Were you kipping, mum?

MUM: Me? I don't sleep properly now. Robert, you know I
    haven't slept for fifteen years.

BOB: That's what I reckoned. Thought: little noise'll draw her
    nose out here, like a priest to whisky, eh mum?

MUM: The phone went, Robert, when you went out.

BOB: Maureen was it?

MUM: Well, she's –

BOB: Didn't you tell that slag what the time is? I bet she's up
    having a right laugh without me.

MUM: It was Janet Morris who I spoke to.

BOB: Eh?

MUM: Oh, Janet's down with Maureen, looking after her for us.
    In Brighton.

BOB: Where? She's meant to be recovering from me. In Norfolk.
    With her sister.

MUM: Robert, you see dear –

BOB: Brighton, you silly woman. You just don't know where you
    are.

MUM: She's gone there . . . without telling you.

BOB: For God's sake, mum, talk straight up, will yer? Do we have
    to wade through all this!

DEL: Bobby!

MUM: Derek, there's a good boy, you explain to him for me. I
    can't. She's had it taken away.

DEL: What did you say?

MUM: Their baby.

DEL: Abortion?

MUM: That word turns me.

DEL: I didn't know she was –

BOB: Eh? What are you on about? Who said she'd had that?

MUM: Robert, she'll say. She'll explain when she gets back.

BOB: I won't wait. You tell me. You know. You tell me, old bag. I feed you. Don't I do everything for you now?

DEL: (*To* BOB) Oh, shut up.

MUM: He's always like this.

BOB: Eh?

MUM: Oh, this is no world for a new child to grow up in.

BOB: The world? It's the bloody same. Stupidity on stilts. What's –

MUM: And you, Robert; you –

BOB: Ah. Now it's me.

MUM: Robert.

BOB: Suddenly it ain't the world all of a sudden.

MUM: Oh I don't know.

DEL: Go back to bed, Mrs Hibbert, and have a rest. (*Looks at* BOB.)

BOB: All right.

MUM: Yes. I'll go and have a lie down for a couple of hours. (*She goes.*)

BOB: Maureen. That cunt.

DEL: What's going on then?

BOB: I'll really –

DEL: Shut it off a minute will you?

BOB: Spite. She did it out of spite. I can be spiteful. I can cut. I'll cut up her carpet. I'll slash it into strips.

DEL: It's your carpet.

BOB: Whose baby is it?

DEL: I didn't realize –

BOB: No. Thought I'd give you a little shock over Sunday dinner with mum, and that. You know.

DEL: Yeah.

BOB: What's she done while I'm holding fire? It's ash.

DEL: She'll tell you why.

BOB: Get off to bed, Del.

DEL: I'll sit up with you, eh.

(*Pause.*)

BOB: I know what it is.

DEL: Do you?

BOB: I know. Because I'm nothing much, am I? Made nothing of myself, have I? I respect you. We're both proud of you. People round here mention you as an example to tearaways.

DEL: Jesus.

BOB: Head of your department at school. Articles printed.

DEL: That no one ever reads.

BOB: What have I accomplished?

DEL: You can do things.

BOB: You haven't seen me since the old days. Then, you couldn't see the end of all that you could do, could you? But all the time, as you're hardly noticing, things are shutting down. Lights are going off. You know. I've got mum to support, rest of her life. Mo-Mo to care for. This house. And no work. No skill. Just . . . (*He gestures violently.*) She thinks, Mo-Mo reckons – I know her, she's got her finger on what's going down, all right? – another chance cut out, all the worry of another gob to feed . . . Jesus, I'll just slide, go right down. As it is, well, she suspects I'm well rotted.

DEL: Why?

BOB: Why? Because now and again I have these rages that she doesn't . . . well, that scare the daylight out her.

DEL: I'm not surprised she's upset.

BOB: I won't work now. Won't give in. It's all bloody-minded defiance now. They've buggered me long enough. I won't do anything for them. I hate them. I really hate them. (*Pause.*) There's . . . there's this cafe we meet in. Boys. The lads. At the back there's a long table with an oil-cloth on it – not fashion, age – and we're sat there, lunchtimes. The lads all eager for their dinner. Like us at school. Who's got a fag then? Anyone lend us 25p for a bet? Who can see us clear with a bacon sandwich till Friday week? And who can? Hours we're there, till the owner gets in a state, barges out the back to us; he yells: right, right, those that's got cold tea and warm seats – piss off out of it! I was at school with them boys. You were.

DEL: Who are they?

73

BOB: You could run through the register: Ashley, Bareham, Burfoot . . . They can't feed their kids now. The motors we burned up the Orpington bypass in: turned to solid rust in their dad's garage. Those boys, they're mainly patient and placid. More than I'll ever be, I mean. (*Pause.*) That's why she – Now you get off to bed.

DEL: No, I –

BOB: You're half asleep.

DEL: We'll sit up together. It'll be getting light soon.
(*Pause.*)

BOB: Oh, leave us alone five minutes can't you?
(*Pause.*)

DEL: Okay. (*Goes.*)
(BOB *stands there. Opens a beer can. Drinks from it. Throws it violently down. Goes out.*)

SCENE TEN

The past. Outside. DEL *runs on, followed by* BOB.

BOB: Wait a minute. Stop! Stop I said, Del!

DEL: What for?

BOB: Where you think you're gonna run to?

DEL: Eh? Fuck you.

BOB: Hold it. (BOB *holds him.*) Right?

DEL: What?

BOB: Right. Better off here we are, than anywhere. For the minute.

DEL: Bobby.

BOB: What?

DEL: How did it happen?

BOB: Jesus. You should –

DEL: Eh? You tell me.

BOB: You got overactive. Don't ask me why. Prat. Pulled you off the little Indian. At the right time, I thought, else we –

DEL: Yes.

BOB: You did get eager.

74

DEL: What hard boys we are.

BOB: Well. His own fault.

DEL: How's that?

BOB: Don't worry.

DEL: How? How?

BOB: They don't usually fight back.

DEL: So?

BOB: Everyone knows that. Nothing would've happened. We'd have mouthed him down and gone back to the disco. Or up Norwood. I weren't expecting him to crack me round the ear with his suitcase. I didn't predict that did I? (BOB *opens the Indian's wallet. Hands some of the money to* DEL. *He's also holding other parts which belong to the wretched victim.*) Gotta get rid of this stuff – carefully. Or they'll cook our goolies in the frying-pan. He'll have reached help in a minute, right?

DEL: 'Tellin me.

BOB: Now.

DEL: No!

BOB: Here. Stuff all this in the bottom of that bin. Go on. (DEL *lifts the lid.*) I'll keep a watch out. (DEL *looks in.*) Do it! Right at the bottom.

DEL: It's . . .

BOB: What?

DEL: Full of puked-up Chinese dinners.

BOB: Cut it out Del. No time for that.

DEL: Bobby.

BOB: Just get rid of it. (*There's a noise,* DEL *presses the stuff in. They're rooted there in terror.*)

DEL: (*Whispering*) What's that?

BOB: Nothing. (*Pause.*) Don't move.

DEL: It's someone. (*Pause.*)

BOB: Hold it.

DEL: What'll we say?

BOB: Say . . .

DEL: What?

BOB: Say we're waiting for someone to go to the Air Cadets with. And we're late for the Church Parade practice.

DEL: Oh Jesus.

BOB: Right?

DEL: Yes, you're right. Gotta back each other up.

BOB: Yeah.

DEL: Even if they torture us.

BOB: Right.

(*A torch comes on. Followed by . . .* MUM.)
Get down.

DEL: Where?

BOB: Here!

(*Pause.*)

MUM: Robert.

BOB: Oh God.

MUM: Robert, you there? (*Pause.*) Don't muck me about, Robert.

DEL: Mrs Hibbert.

MUM: Derek?

BOB: Hallo mum, having a walk before bed?

MUM: Get home.

BOB: Fuck off.

MUM: You get home at once.

BOB: Mum!

MUM: Robert!

BOB: Leave us alone.

MUM: You only get into trouble.

BOB: What trouble.

MUM: And then I can't bloody sleep.

BOB: Mum you've been at work all day.

MUM: I know that. Don't tell me that.

BOB: Go to bed then.

MUM: Derek your dad's up and wild. He'll give you a hiding when you get back.

DEL: Yes, I – (*He begins to move away.*)

BOB: Wait a minute, Del. Why can't we do what we want? (*Suddenly* MUM *grabs* BOB's *hair and pulls his head down.*)

MUM: Don't –

BOB: Don't pull my hair!

MUM: Don't make my life a misery!

BOB: Del, get the bag off me.

DEL: Oh leave him, Mrs Hibbert.

MUM: (*To* BOB) You little animal. You blasted creature! I never cared much if you didn't like me. Don't want a lot of people liking me –

BOB: Not one person I can think of likes you!

MUM: Why do I need it? I never liked my old parents. Till later. Too late. But they liked me. And I like you. But don't you –

BOB: Mum!

MUM: Hurt me!

BOB: No, mum, no, never, no!

    (*She lets him go. He stands up straight.*)

    I should have hit you.

MUM: The police were round.

DEL: What?

BOB: When?

DEL: What did they want?

BOB: What time were they round?

    (*She walks away.*)

    Mum! Mum! What's happening?

MUM: I knew you two had been mucking about. I knew it.

DEL: You mean –

MUM: Next time, they will get you.

BOB: You liar. Bloody liar, that's what you are!

MUM: They will. Now come on. Come home. (*Pause.*) Come home.

    (*They go off.*)

SCENE ELEVEN

The present. BOB *on stage, eating a piece of toast, cup of coffee in other hand. It is morning.* DEL *on his knees, crawling up behind* BOB.

DEL: (*Hoarse*) Bobby.

BOB: Morning.

77

DEL: Bobby boy.

(BOB *turns*.)

BOB: Del, my son. Yer legs have gone?

DEL: From the waist down.

BOB: You woke up crippled?

DEL: Never be able to walk for charity again. No future.

BOB: 'Cept in modelling wheelchairs. (BOB *pours a little coffee over*
     DEL's *head*.) Little man don't blubber.

DEL: Oh stop it!

(BOB *laughs*. DEL *stands up*. DEL *takes Bob's toast. Has a bite.*
Gives it back.)

You haven't slept?

BOB: This afternoon.

DEL: You'll get –

BOB: I'm okay.

DEL: Bob, I want to get back soon.

BOB: Why's that?

DEL: I've got a lot of marking to do, for tomorrow. For my first
     class in fact.

BOB: Monday, I s'pose.

DEL: Exactly.

BOB: What'll we do today?

DEL: No.

BOB: Eh?

DEL: I think I'd like to say goodbye.

BOB: It's early.

DEL: You let me oversleep.

(MUM *comes on*.)

Morning, Mrs Hibbert.

MUM: Hallo, Derek.

DEL: What are you going to do today?

MUM: Sit down.

DEL: Good idea.

(DEL *takes Bob's toast and has a chew. Hands it back*. BOB
offers it to MUM. *She shakes her head*.)

BOB: Wait a minute then: I'll boil you an egg, mum.

MUM: I'll –

BOB: Are you hungry?

78

MUM: I'll –

BOB: (*To* DEL) Can you ever hear what she's saying?

MUM: I'll book myself into a home, I think.

BOB: You've got a home.

MUM: I don't know.

DEL: Don't say that, Mrs Hibbert.

MUM: Why not?

DEL: You're not old.

MUM: No, I think I should.

DEL: You're . . . loved.

BOB: Mum? More than most. She's bloody cherished.

MUM: My back's gone. I'm gone, now. You don't understand yet.
      I'm like them deck-chairs that we used to have.

BOB: Mum. I'll boil you an egg and you'll stop moaning five
      minutes. Give us all a breather.

MUM: Young people, growing up. Don't want to be in the way
      now.

DEL: Silly.

MUM: I'll get worse. (*Indicating* BOB.) And him like he is.

BOB: Now, now, mum.

DEL: What d'you mean?

BOB: Don't get her started.

DEL: Mrs Hibbert, d'you want to tell me?

MUM: Not working any more. Seeing me in the day when he comes
      in from . . . I get such looks from him. You should see him.
      Especially if Maureen's not here to say something. (*Pause. To*
      BOB.) I know where you go.

BOB: So what, mum?

MUM: Oh yes, Derek, I know him. Up roaming about that dirty
      waste-ground he is.

BOB: Mum.

MUM: I saw it bombed. Mr Jarman was killed up there that night. I
      know the sort Robert meets. What they are. I know their . . .
      mums. Oh yes, oh yes. I don't go along with it either. I lived
      through the war; I know what's what.

BOB: You know everything. Funny you're not in the Cabinet.

MUM: (*To* DEL) So I've booked myself in already. It's a lovely place.

DEL: So is this, Mrs Hibbert.

MUM: (*To* BOB) I don't like eggs. Fancy offering me eggs. What a thought! I don't think I've eaten an egg since 1942. Who do you think I am? How long have we lived here together? (*The doorbell rings*.)

DEL: Shall I answer it?

MUM: No, I'm off that way now. (*She goes off*.)

BOB: What a bastard you are.

DEL: What?

BOB: Oh yes. I must be insane not to have noticed.

DEL: What are you saying?

BOB: It's Maureen dragged you down here. To look the loony over, eh? I should have recognized the icy style of it.

DEL: I'm always like this.

BOB: You piss off, and then you come back poking yer nose into my life.

(MAUREEN *comes on, with* MUM.)

Maureen.

MAUREEN: Yes.

BOB: How d'you feel?

MAUREEN: What are you on about, Bobby?

(*Pause*.)

BOB: Don't stand there. Get off yer feet a minute.

MAUREEN: Don't shout about the place.

BOB: I'm not.

(DEL *takes her suitcase*.)

DEL: This is heavy.

MAUREEN: Derek.

DEL: Hi.

MAUREEN: (*To* DEL) D'you think –

DEL: What?

MAUREEN: D'you think he'll ever work, Del? You've seen him. Have you asked him? Did you discuss it? What d'you think of your old friend?

DEL: The job situation. It's pretty bad.

MAUREEN: Oh yes.

BOB: Where's the baby?

MAUREEN: You're concerned about something.

BOB: Maureen, answer me.

80

MAUREEN: What'd we do with it anyway? We wouldn't survive together, the three of us.

BOB: What are we doing? Killing to survive? That the latest idea she's got?

MUM: Robert. Quiet, quiet, now. Don't talk about it.

MAUREEN: (*To* DEL) Good weekend?

DEL: We had quite a time.

MAUREEN: Look like you did.

DEL: Yeah, well . . .

MAUREEN: Look like you did. I've seen the kitchen.

BOB: Mo-Mo, can I get you anything?

MAUREEN: Total anaesthetic?

BOB: Oh yeah, I'll dash right out and –

MAUREEN: Tired of him. I'm tired of this man. I can't tell you. I won't bother to.

BOB: . . . And get my biggest hammer.

MAUREEN: (*To* DEL) Have you ever been to Brighton?

DEL: Mo?

MAUREEN: It's got in me, his germ; got right behind my eyeballs it has. Bobby brought me down, over months when I wasn't looking. Didn't you? I didn't see how it could be happening. You feel low and that. Get weaker. It's like you been crying a lot. I tell you Derek, mum knows what I'm on about, I was opening out at the bloody seams, I mean it. Then it dawned on me. I'm a bit slow, you know me.

BOB: Give it a wait, will yer.

MAUREEN: It was his gloom that did for me. And his violence, I nearly forgot. (*She laughs.*) Not that he clouted me. Just that it filled the place. Every time you breathed in . . . you just about got a lungful of lead, like.

BOB: Shut up.

MAUREEN: (*To* DEL) It's the gospel, what I've given you. I'm glad I got away. Had to. To clean myself, clean myself. Jesus, if you'd been here when . . . (*To* BOB) What d'you do all day?

BOB: Del knows. All weekend we've beaten that meat.

MAUREEN: (*To* BOB) What d'you do?

BOB: Don't. (*Pause.*) I . . . walk about.

MAUREEN: He's well exercised; yes.

BOB: Okay?

MAUREEN: You're right. It is what you do. Now and again you sniff at things, as well. You get right fed up to the teeth.

BOB: You're right – I do. I do. You know why I do.

MAUREEN: You want something to happen don't you? A brick goes through a window, eh, don't it? Or you poke yer prick through a Paki's letter-box don't you? And they can hear you, the family, can't they, dribbling on their hall lino, as they're having their tea.

DEL: There's a whole machinery down on him, Mo. You've got to see that.

MAUREEN: I'm tired. I don't want to understand. The more I see the further away everything gets. (*To* BOB.) A baby. What'd that be?

BOB: What?

MAUREEN: Something I look after. You'd be useless. Not interested, after five minutes. I don't want all that. Nor does your mum.

BOB: Mo-Mo –

MAUREEN: Now you –

BOB: Maureen!

MAUREEN: Just listen! (*Pause.*) Oh, crawl out this place. Walk out, I mean. That's quicker. Do it now, too. Get right away from me. Till I can bear you again. I don't know when that'll be. I hate to think.

BOB: Mum. Hear what she's saying to me in your house?

MUM: Oh don't turn to me now.

BOB: Just to explain.

DEL: She's not well.

MUM: (*To* BOB) I've heard your voice a thousand times.

BOB: Mum, weren't you right, what you said about her. She's a pushy bitch. Take everything, you said.

MAUREEN: Leave her alone.

BOB: Listen mum. Tell her . . . she's taken life. The baby. Ours, and that. You know what she's done.

MUM: You.

BOB: Eh?

MUM: Don't I know all about you?

82

BOB: What are you saying?

MUM: Oh get out of my sight.

(BOB *stares at her. Silence.* BOB *moves away*.)

DEL: Bob. (*Pause.*) Bobby boy.

BOB: Bastard. (BOB *leaves. Pause.*)

MAUREEN: I'm sore.

MUM: Are you?

MAUREEN: I do feel bad.

MUM: Do you? (MUM *looks at her*.) Yes, I expect you will, for a time, Mo.

MAUREEN: Yes, 'course I will. If you do something like that, you must expect . . .

MUM: I'm very glad to have you back home, Maureen dear.

MAUREEN: Oh, are you mum? Are you?

MUM: Only realized it when you came in. Without you here –

MAUREEN: What was it like? Were they –

MUM: It was like . . . I kept thinking of . . . it was getting like it was then . . . They kept – oh I don't know now. (*To* DEL.) D'you know what I mean?

DEL: Yes.

(MAUREEN *laughs*.)

MAUREEN: (*To* MUM) Well, have a rest now.

(MUM *strokes* MAUREEN's *hair*.)

MUM: I will, don't worry. But you must.

MAUREEN: You know, you're not off anywhere, mum. I've decided I won't hear any more of that leaving business.

MUM: (*To* DEL) Only thought better to leave the two of them to each other.

MAUREEN: Oh thanks! Who says we want to be together? You stay here between us, where you bloody belong!

MUM: We'll see.

MAUREEN: See what?

MUM: How he . . . how Robert behaves himself from now on.

MAUREEN: You just stay. Eh, Del?

DEL: No. Not if he's upsetting her.

MUM: Let's not talk about it.

MAUREEN: I'll see to him, I will. My energy'll be up soon. There'll be no more contamination from him. He might be a bit desperate and that. But I won't be scared of that little bastard. I'll see to him. (*Pause. To* DEL.) That's enough about us. What are you doing?

DEL: Me?

MAUREEN: You still at that place?

DEL: No, I'm leaving the school in the summer.

MAUREEN: Why's that?

DEL: Been offered a good – very good job.

MUM: More money and everything?

DEL: That kind of thing. Outside London. Near Oxford actually.

MUM: University?

DEL: No.

MAUREEN: D'you want to go away that far?

DEL: I can't wait.

MUM: Oh, that's lovely.

MAUREEN: You've got to go on to other things, haven't you?

DEL: Yes, it can change you.

MAUREEN: Otherwise you stay the same.

DEL: Well, yes – (*He is about to go.*)

MUM: Derek. Here.

(DEL *moves towards her.*)

Don't make nothing up now, just tell me what you make of my little boy, seeing him again after . . .

(DEL *gestures.*)

D'you remember when he wanted to get tattooed?

DEL: God, yes. I expect he feels embarrassed now.

MAUREEN: It looks bloody rich, never mind hilarious, I can tell you.

MUM: Oh I didn't realize he'd actually gone out and done it.

DEL: Yes.

MAUREEN: Oh mum.

DEL: Listen. I'm sorry. I think I'd better get off now.

MAUREEN: Thanks Del.

DEL: Mrs Hibbert.

MUM: Bye Derek.

(DEL *leaves.*)

MAUREEN: Would you, Mum –

MUM: Eh?

MAUREEN: Have liked a little baby about the place?

84

MUM: A baby.

MAUREEN: Would you, honestly?

MUM: Baby. He's one. We've got one in this house already.

MAUREEN: Don't say what I want to hear. Tell the truth for Christ's sake! (*Pause.*)

MUM: Oh let me get the kettle on. Bring you a brandy too, if you like. I hid the bottle from them two.

MAUREEN: No, you sit down.

MUM: I've just got up.

MAUREEN: Doesn't matter.

MUM: Wait a minute. (*She moves away. Stops.*) Tell you.

MAUREEN: Eh?

MUM: Mo, dear. Tell you what I say . . .

MAUREEN: What's that then?

MUM: You interested?

MAUREEN: Why d'you say that? 'Course I'm interested. Why d'you think I'm –

MUM: What I think –

MAUREEN: Yes?

MUM: Shit to them.

MAUREEN: Mum?

MUM: Yes. Yes, all right! What about me? What about you? What about us? It's taken me long enough to realize. Taken me all my life to get clear. I'm in this state because of it.

MAUREEN: What state, mum?

MUM: Oh you know. And I say shit on their bloody faces.

MAUREEN: Well I'll drink to that.

MUM: You should, dear. (MUM *kisses her.*) You did the right thing.

MAUREEN: Did I?

MUM: Sometimes I wish I'd done the same. I know it's wicked to say that. But I think it. I do.

MAUREEN: Do you?

MUM: Oh yes, I know I do.
    (*Pause.*)

MAUREEN: Mum shall we . . . d'you want to go out?

MUM: Out?

MAUREEN: You and me. Together.

MUM: Where?

85

MAUREEN: We'll get out tonight, if you like.

MUM: Where is there now?

MAUREEN: Don't worry about that. When I'm feeling a bit better, later on, I'll ring for a car to take us to the ABC. See a film or something, eh? Then we can get something to eat. Walk a little way. Anything could happen.

MUM: I'd like to.

MAUREEN: Would you?

MUM: Enjoy ourselves.

MAUREEN: Yes, for once.

MUM: Why not?

MAUREEN: Right. We'll do that.

MUM: Yeah. We'll do that.

(MUM *moves away*.

MAUREEN *holds her stomach and groans*.)

SCENE TWELVE

The past. DEL *on stage.* BOB *comes on.*

BOB: Del?

DEL: Yeah.

BOB: There you are.

DEL: Yeah. I've . . .

BOB: Eh?

DEL: Just mowed all this bloody lawn. Dad insisted on these superb stripes.

BOB: Just fuck the lawn, eh?

DEL: If you like.

BOB: Coming out or what?

DEL: Oh I don't know. My arms feel a bit . . . tired.

BOB: Eh?

DEL: Yeah.

BOB: What you doing then? Going in?

DEL: I'm not sure.

BOB: Don't muck about. Haven't seen you for a while. Haven't told you about the job.

DEL: No, you haven't.

BOB: Well say what you want, idiot, and we can do it.

DEL: I've said.

BOB: What?

DEL: I don't know.

BOB: You been to the dentist?

DEL: Me?

BOB: You're a bit shook up. All shook, I'd say.

DEL: Am I? Yeah, I am. Am I?

BOB: The lawn-mower must have bin vibrating.

DEL: No. Hey, I read in the paper and that.

BOB: Oh yeah. Did you?

    (*Pause.*)

DEL: Yeah I read it.

BOB: Well.

DEL: 'Course I bloody read it!

BOB: I expected you to.

DEL: 'Bout who they found down by –

BOB: All right.

DEL: We won't be caught.

BOB: I don't know.

DEL: We won't. He hardly saw –

BOB: Our faces.

DEL: Well he didn't. We jumped on him from behind, remember, under the motorway. There's no light there.

BOB: I saw his mug.

DEL: Did you?

BOB: Yes, when you – I wish we'd –

DEL: Oh don't go on about it.

    (*Pause.*)

BOB: You staying in tonight again?

DEL: Yeah, I am, I reckon.

BOB: Oh Del. Come on.

DEL: Think I'd better.

BOB: Oh yeah?

DEL: What?

BOB: I don't think you are. (BOB *lifts* DEL *up, from behind.*)

DEL: What you doing?

87

BOB: I reckon we'll go out.

DEL: Bob, leave it out will you.

BOB: Come on. Here we go.

DEL: You bloody idiot, no wonder they expelled you.

BOB: Up by the Crystal Palace Tower!

DEL: Bobby, you bastard!

(MUM *comes on*.)

MUM: What a day I've had of it. I'm running that shop on me own practically now, I am. What you two diddling about at now?

BOB: Weighing him.

MUM: What d'you weigh, Derek?

DEL: Christ knows.

MUM: Put him down now.

(BOB *drops him*.)

BOB: What a body.

MUM: Don't hurt him.

BOB: Why not? He's getting uppity.

MUM: They found a bloke hurt down by the motorway over there.

BOB: Did they? Yeah, I know about that.

DEL: Did they, Mrs Hibbert?

MUM: Some poor little sod, crawling about, kicked and that.

BOB: We've read it.

DEL: Yeah.

MUM: Doubt if they'll catch the beasts. That kind of violence. So many people'd knock over a Paki for nothing, these days.

BOB: Mum, what you come over Del's for now?

MUM: Oh Julie's out again. And who d'you think's sitting in my kitchen right at this moment?

BOB: That Jehovah's Witness come round again?

MUM: No. Maureen.

BOB: I didn't know she was coming round.

MUM: Thought she'd drop in on you, didn't she.

BOB: Well she can wait five minutes. Del and me were just off out.

MUM: She's eating my biscuits.

DEL: Do you get on with Maureen, Mrs Hibbert?

MUM: Oh you know.

BOB: Do you?

MUM: (*To* DEL) You know what mums are like. I'd always be a bit

88

jealous, whoever it was. No one's good enough for my boy.
(*She cuddles* BOB. *To* DEL.) He's my baby.

DEL: Big idiot.

MUM: (*To* BOB) He loves me. Say you love your mum.

BOB: Mum, I'm crazy about you.

MUM: Are you? Why don't you ever touch that banjo?

BOB: Mum, don't wear me nerves out.

MUM: You can talk about that. (*Pause*.) I'll get back to Maureen.
You coming?

BOB: Give us a minute will you? Don't follow me about
everywhere. I've told you about that.

MUM: I can't help it.

BOB: Well try.

(MUM *moves away*.)

Hey. Tell Maureen we're not married. Not yet. Right?

MUM: Don't leave me with her too long. I've got things to get on with.

BOB: Go on then.

(MUM *goes*.)

Well, dull arse?

DEL: Maureen.

BOB: Yeah.

DEL: The telephonist from Telephone House.

BOB: Yeah. No. Don't run her down. We go out to these good
places and that. That's why you haven't seen me much.

DEL: What's the job like?

BOB: Good. Good.

DEL: Is it?

BOB: Not bad.

DEL: I noticed you been looking a bit smart lately. Out with your
new friends. I got off the train at Peckham Rye last Saturday.
You didn't see me. And there you were. With the lads. You
like the lads. You did look casual. Where were you going?

BOB: They're good boys. In my line. We talk about technical stuff.

DEL: What – bras?

BOB: Cars and that. Engines. Exhausts.

DEL: You name it – I don't know about it, eh?

BOB: Del, I didn't want you to feel excluded. So I didn't invite you
to come out, you know.

89

DEL: Don't worry.

BOB: No. I better go.

DEL: Oh. 'Course. Hope Maureen hasn't put on too much weight, waiting.

BOB: Don't worry about her. (*Pause.*) Well?

DEL: Don't go now if you don't have to. We could talk.

BOB: No, I think I'd better shift. She'll tell me off.

DEL: Okay. Yeah, sure.

BOB: You all right then?

DEL: I'm fine.

BOB: Don't –

DEL: What?

BOB: Try not to think about it.

DEL: I do.

BOB: Yeah. I do.

DEL: You see.

BOB: I know what you mean.

DEL: Good.

BOB: (*About to go*) Well, I –

DEL: I want to get out of South London.

BOB: Do you?

DEL: I want that badly. I think about it all the time. Getting away. Don't you?

BOB: Make a run for it, eh?

DEL: No. Plan a way. Properly. (*Pause.*) I've decided. And I'll carry it through. I feel better for having decided. I'm going to teacher training.

BOB: Are you, clever boy?

DEL: Yeah, because I can't stand it any more. And if I had a mother like yours –

BOB: Del, I must go.

DEL: I'd run a mile.

BOB: Hey. (*Pause.*) Oh Jesus. Bye. (*Pause.*) Hey.

DEL: What?

BOB: I'll probably kill myself when I'm thirty!
(BOB *runs off.*
DEL *remains on stage.*
Blackout.)

BORDERLINE

You have navigated with raging soul far from the paternal home, passing beyond the sea's double rocks, and you now inhabit a foreign land.

Medea

Characters

AMJAD
ANWAR
WHITE NEIGHBOUR
HAROON
ANIL
FAROUK
BANOO
YASMIN
RAVI
SUSAN
VALERIE
AMINA
BILL

Borderline was performed at the Royal Court Theatre, London, after a short tour, in a production by Joint Stock Theatre Group, on 2nd November 1981. The cast was as follows:

AMJAD ANWAR WHITE NEIGHBOUR	David Beames
HAROON ANIL FAROUK	Vincent Ebrahim
BANOO YASMIN	Deborah Findlay
RAVI	Nizwar Karanj
SUSAN VALERIE	Lesley Manville
AMINA	Rita Wolf
BILL	Michael Lightfoot

Director	Max Stafford-Clark
Designer	Peter Hartwell
Lighting	Hugh Laver

Act One

Behind Amina's house. AMINA *runs on. She is wearing salwar kamiz.*

AMJAD: (*Off*) Amina! Banoo! Where's Amina? Banoo!

AMINA: (*To* HAROON) Come on. Round here. Haroon I want to
    talk to you.

    (HAROON *comes on. He's carrying books.*)

HAROON: Amina.

AMINA: Come on, it's all right.

    (*He moves closer to her.*)

    Put your books down. (*Pause.*) Go on.

    (*He does so.*)

    Good. Let's have it.

HAROON: No.

AMINA: Let's have it now.

HAROON: No, we can't now, Amina.

AMINA: Why not?

HAROON: Not against the wall in the alley behind your house and
    everything. Not when your father's shouting for his tea. Don't
    people have it in bed any more?

AMINA: We had it in my parents' bed when they went to Walsall.

HAROON: Yeah. A year ago.

AMINA: You got on me. Whenever you looked round, that
    photograph of dad on the dressing-table looked back at you. It
    scared you.

HAROON: I couldn't come.

AMINA: You couldn't.

HAROON: He blocked me, the old bastard.

AMINA: He's not here now.

HAROON: He's just there in the house. I can practically smell him.

AMINA: We've fucked in worse places. Your eyes are red.

HAROON: Are they? I've been studying night and day, Amina.
    That's where I've been.

AMINA: But are you learning anything?

97

HAROON: I don't know, I don't know. I'm reading all the time. I can't remember anything though.

AMINA: Sounds like you've got the taps on but you haven't put the plug in.

HAROON: That's it.

AMINA: I think of you working when I'm at work.

HAROON: Do you Amina?

AMINA: And in the evenings sitting there with Mum and Dad.

HAROON: Good, great. (*Pause.*) You'd better go now.

AMINA: And I'm quite happy today.

HAROON: Why?

AMINA: To be with you and that.

HAROON: That's good.

AMINA: Good?

HAROON: Very good.

AMINA: Don't you know what these eighteen months we've been going out have been like? I've risked every bloody thing.

HAROON: I know that.

AMINA: That hopping in and out of my bedroom window. My mother caught me with my leg over the sill last week. I said I was doing a dance exercise. Things aren't easy for me. And you're all I've got.

HAROON: Same for me, Amina.

AMINA: It's never the same for boys.

HAROON: Hey, I can hear –

AMINA: What?

HAROON: Sounds like your old man bellowing. I can practically hear his legs swelling up with rage and everything .

AMJAD: (*Off*) Amina!

AMINA: Oh Dad, don't shout all the time.

HAROON: Shhh . . . he can hear through walls.

AMINA: Today his legs are up like melons. He says he's like a general, shouting orders to me and mum from his chair.

HAROON: Heart disease, your old man's got. My father calls it the English disease.

AMINA: Why?

HAROON: The English get bad hearts because they have rotten souls and bad consciences.

98

AMINA: I think the food your old man's restaurant serves gives people disease. More people have died screaming after eating a meat vindaloo . . .

HAROON: All right, Amina.

AMINA: Anyway, Dad's Pakistani. He can't have any English disease.

HAROON: He's so pale with illness he could be mistaken for English.

AMINA: Haroon. I want to ask you. Just tell me if you don't like it when I talk in a free way.

HAROON: I'm used to it. You like words like 'fuck'. You think they're dangerous.

AMINA: I know, I'm evil, aren't I? I'm only like it with you. Usually I'm a quiet ghost – I'm there but I'm not. I can't help myself. (*Pointing to his crotch.*) It's gone up again.

HAROON: For Christ's sake it hasn't. It's my revision notes. And the third chapter of my novel and everything. (*He takes out a roll of papers. He glances through it.*)

AMINA: You can still fuck me if you like. In the garden behind your father's restaurant.

HAROON: The waiters go out there to smoke and gossip about my brother.

AMINA: What about the offices of the Asian Youth Front?

HAROON: Anwar's called a meeting to discuss the attacks. Anwar and Yasmin are looking for me. Trying to force me to write something on how to prepare for the invasion those animals have been threatening. I'm sick of the Youth Front pressuring me. You're the only person I can talk to and everything.

AMINA: And I'm a terrible person. My mother would die. My father would throttle me, he would. I have nightmares about him finding out about us, that we kiss and do it.

HAROON: Don't mention me – even if he pulls your teeth out.

AMINA: When he's ill and asks for his Koran, his yellow eyes go into me. I think, 'He knows, he can see what I'm like.'

AMJAD: (*Off*) Amina. Tea and sandwiches!

HAROON: Go to him – quick. If we're caught he'll get you married.

AMINA: I deserve it. (*As he goes.*) You still on me then?

HAROON: What do you think's here in this place for me?

AMINA: Me. (*Pause.*) You'll leave I s'pose.

HAROON: Can you see me taking over my father's restaurant?

AMINA: When your exams are over go to college in London. It's not far.

HAROON: Not far enough. I really need to smash the connection and everything.

AMINA: We've got on for so long.

HAROON: The future's longer. Bound to be when you're eighteen.

AMINA: I can get out Thursday.

HAROON: Up the car park then.

AMINA: Haroon.

HAROON: What?

AMINA: Don't leave.

HAROON: We'll see.

AMINA: Don't leave.

HAROON: Amina.

AMINA: Don't leave.

HAROON: This place and the past, it's like an octopus. You drag one limb off you while another's curled itself round you.
(*He goes.*)

AMJAD: Amina!

AMINA: All right, dad, I'm coming.

SCENE TWO

The coach to London. The journalist SUSAN *sitting in the bus. She's reading James Morris's 'Farewell the Trumpets'.* RAVI, *carrying his bags, approaches.*

RAVI: Does this bus go to London?

SUSAN: Yes, I think so.

RAVI: I'll sit here then, shall I?

SUSAN: Yes.

RAVI: This is my first time in England. I'm a complete stranger.

SUSAN: Why don't you sit by the window then.

RAVI: If you could.

(*They swop.*)

My first view of England.

SUSAN: I'd keep my eyes closed if I were you. We were on the same flight I think, from Bombay.

RAVI: Were we?

SUSAN: Just let me tell you I loved the subcontinent.

RAVI: Good.

SUSAN: D'you know, when we flew over Slough I nearly burst into tears. I didn't want to come back.

RAVI: Did you have a good holiday?

SUSAN: No, I'm a journalist. I'll be using some of the material I gathered in India to make a radio programme.

RAVI: Oh very nice.

SUSAN: What a fuss they make of you over there.

RAVI: Oh yes.

SUSAN: You play a game of tennis and you have an umpire and two ball boys magnetized by your every move. You ride for miles in a rickshaw dragged by a skinny fifty-year-old father of seven and you feel so guilty you give him two years' wages for a tip. If your tea's cold and you complain some poor boy is kicked out of a job and his grandmother starves to death. It's difficult not to find yourself becoming some kind of fatuous aristocrat.

RAVI: You were well treated in India?

SUSAN: Too well. (*Pause.*) Where are you going?

RAVI: London.

SUSAN: Where will you stay?

RAVI: Oh, London. I have the address of my friend Anil. The English people all seem very busy to me.

SUSAN: Do they?

RAVI: Yes. look there, in that shop. They're standing in the window, selling things like mad.

SUSAN: Where? No, they're not real, they're dummies. It's a boutique, a clothes shop.

RAVI: The trees go completely brown here, I've heard.

SUSAN: In the winter.

RAVI: And the houses are small here. The people look – small.

SUSAN: Did you expect more size?

RAVI: They ruled in my country for so long, I thought they'd be bigger. I hope Anil got my letter. I haven't seen him for five years. He writes to his wife in my town that he's very lonely in Ealing. Will you tell me when we've arrived in Ealing, so I can get off?

SUSAN: No, you'll have to change at Victoria.

RAVI: This bus doesn't go to Ealing?

SUSAN: No.

RAVI: Where am I going then?

SUSAN: Victoria.

RAVI: Victoria? I'll ask there, then. I have his address.

SUSAN: Listen. Here's my phone number. My name's Susan, by the way.

RAVI: I'm Ravi.

SUSAN: Ravi, you call me if you're in any trouble. In India people treated me marvellously. And I'm interested in making a programme about the lives of Asians in the mother country. I'd like to see how you get on.

RAVI: Before I left, Anil's uncle gave me advice. He said, 'When you meet English girls, always say, first thing, always say, first thing . . .'

SUSAN: What?

RAVI: Oh no.

SUSAN: Go on. What was it?

RAVI: Oh no. It was basic advice. What are those people waiting for there?

SUSAN: There? I think it's a dole queue, the unemployed.

SCENE THREE

AMJAD, *Amina's father, sitting at home. He smokes furiously and is dressed shabbily, long johns sticking out of the bottom of his trousers. In contrast his wife,* BANOO, *always dresses well.* AMJAD *is obviously sick.*

AMJAD: (*Still shouting*) Amina! Banoo! Amina!
   (*Pause.* BANOO *comes in.*)

BANOO: Amjad, did you call for something?

102

AMJAD: Banoo. Banoo, where's my Amina?

BANOO: Making tea. She's been lying down upstairs, I think. Poor little thing, she's got cystitis. It's the cold in the supermarket.

AMJAD: I've been shouting for an hour. My heart's on its last legs. My tea's the only thing I look forward to. You make me shout like a child for it.

BANOO: I've been in the kitchen with the door closed.

AMJAD: Aren't you working in the bedroom? I can't hear the sewing machine, Banoo.

BANOO: Amjad, it's broken again.

AMJAD: But you've done nothing this week. The boy will be coming to collect the garments tomorrow. Why did you break it?

BANOO: It's not my fault. It's faulty.

AMJAD: Make them pay for it.

BANOO: I know they won't. You have to wait for the hire-people to come and fix it. And we're paid so little for our work.

AMJAD: Your face is beginning to look like an old turnip. I wonder why? You tell me you're working but you're secretly wailing – thinking about Pakistan, your village, your blasted mother. I've bought this house.

BANOO: Yes, Amjad.

AMJAD: Every foot of wood I sweated for in the bakery. Now every woodworm and insect in it I'll fight for with my last legs.

BANOO: I think we should go back.

AMJAD: Don't start this argument again. You can't leave a place because you don't like a few people's faces.

BANOO: Amjad, it's not the faces. It's the bricks and stones through the window. And we're afraid to go out.

AMJAD: Well stay in.

BANOO: Our lives are a misery.

AMJAD: I've been a superb husband to you.

BANOO: Oh yes.

AMJAD: Superb. No wife could expect more. I won't run. You have to stand up for things.

BANOO: But you can't stand, Amjad – your legs are so swollen.

AMJAD: What? (*Pause.*) Amina!

BANOO: She's not well.

(AMINA *comes in bearing tea.*)

AMJAD: Look – my daughter! She's very well. Her innocent face. Good girl, Amina.

AMINA: I fell asleep for a few minutes Papa. I've been working so hard. (*She puts down the tea and starts to go.*)

AMJAD: Amina. Here. Come here.

AMINA: No, Papa.

AMJAD: Yes, yes! Here. (*He pulls her cheek quite violently.*) You know I think you're a lovely girl.

AMINA: Well I am.

AMJAD: You are, hey? Hey?

BANOO: Leave her, poor girl.

AMJAD: Don't tell me to leave my own baby girl. The others are there in Pakistan. They're so happy without their father. I can pull my own daughter, can't I? I love her.

AMINA: Papa, let me bring in the washing. Your shirts are there.

AMJAD: Good girl. Is it raining again?

BANOO: Has it started to rain?

AMJAD: She said it has.

AMINA: Mama, why do you like the rain?

BANOO: When it rains there's less people on the road. Then I like to go out. I take my umbrella and do the shopping.

AMINA: Is that why you like the rain, Mama?

AMJAD: Is that a jam sandwich you've made me, my Amina?

BANOO: Then I feel free.

AMJAD: Pass it here.

(AMINA *passes him the sandwiches.*)

BANOO: You can be out, but you're alone.

AMJAD: Have you used margarine?

AMINA: No, papa.

AMJAD: (*Friendly*) I know you eat margarine, Amina. You did at school. You do in your work canteen. You're that margarine-eating type, aren't you?

AMINA: Sometimes you can't help it papa.

AMJAD: There's pigs' fat in it.

AMINA: (*Laughing*) No, Papa.

BANOO: No, Amjad, I don't think they put that.

AMJAD: Woman. What did you say?

BANOO: I said I don't think there's pigs' fat in margarine.

AMJAD: What do you know, woman? Except how to contradict me, which after long years of practice you're an expert at? I can't say anything in this house without being in the wrong. Is there anyone in England more in the wrong than me?

BANOO: No, Amjad.

AMJAD: (*To* AMINA, *who's quietly laughing at all this*) Pass me another sandwich. Don't snort like a horse. Why were you late home from work? Were you kissing a boy?

BANOO: Amjad!

AMJAD: I'm joking, Banoo. Did those boys call you Paki in the park?

AMINA: Not today, Papa.

AMJAD: Tell me the truth, or I'll never let you work again.

BANOO: Amjad, she does so much for the family.

AMJAD: (*To* AMINA) Why were you late?

AMINA: They kept us at work.

BANOO: Why?

AMINA: To search our bags for thieving.

AMJAD: They paid you?

AMINA: Yes Papa.

AMJAD: Give your mother your wages before you go to bed.

AMINA: I always do Papa.

AMJAD: Good girl then.

BANOO: (*To* AMINA) Are you cutting the onions?

AMINA: Yes, I'll see to it now.

BANOO: And soak the lentils for tomorrow.

AMINA: Shall I help you sewing this evening?

AMJAD: She's broken the machine.

BANOO: (*To* AMINA) Come and sit with me this evening. I don't like you in your room all the time. Don't you like being with us?

AMJAD: Of course she does.

AMINA: Yes.

BANOO: You always seem to have other things on your mind these days. Come and talk to me about work. I'm so ignorant about these things. But I like it when you tell me what you're doing. We used to be so close.

AMJAD: Banoo, wait. Amina, come here.

BANOO: Now you never tell us what you think.

AMINA: I don't think any more.

AMJAD: Amina, what – ?

BANOO: (*To* AMINA, *despite* AMJAD's *interruptions*) Why not?

AMINA: It's no use. Things carry you along.

BANOO: Oh Amina, that's not a good attitude.

AMJAD: Amina, what colour do you want the kitchen?

BANOO: I know it's difficult for you here.

AMINA: Sometimes.

BANOO: It's the same for all of us. For Papa. And for me.

AMINA: I feel sorry for what you have to put up with.

BANOO: I don't want you feeling sorry. I want you to help me understand. But anyway, I understand more things about you than you think.

AMJAD: Amina, what colour do you want the kitchen?

AMINA: I don't know Papa. What things?

BANOO: Oh yes.

AMINA: Mama, that's frightening.

AMJAD: Please think about the kitchen! We're a family. I can't think about everything myself!

AMINA: Yes Papa, I will think. (*She goes.*)

AMJAD: I feel better today.

BANOO: Oh I'm so happy to hear you say that Amjad.

AMJAD: Banoo, I've analysed our whole problem.

BANOO: What is it then?

AMJAD: you see, Banoo, they're jealous of us, the working class here. We've worked. We've bought this house. We've painted the outside. No one else in the street has done that. They can only pour beer into their fat guts and shave their heads like sandpaper.

BANOO: Think, Amjad, in Pakistan you'd be so loved.

AMJAD: I don't want to be loved by your relatives. I want the kitchen decorated. I'll send you to Pakistan for a holiday after the court case.

BANOO: It takes months.

AMJAD: The law is good here. It's slow. But good.

BANOO: We've been insulted by the neighbours for so long.

AMJAD: You know, I was in the Indian army. I've seen things fall apart. In the Indian army you see nothing else. I've seen men take the law into their own hands. In the Indian army you see nothing else. Keep this to yourself. So you have to rely on solid authority that doesn't shift about. Those two who came here that day. Anwar. And the girl.

BANOO: Yasmin.

AMJAD: Doesn't her father hit her for that? Offering to protect us, with their friends. I threw him out. I told them: go back to nursery school.

BANOO: Amjad, the law wasn't there when the neighbours knocked you down. When the police came they said: go to a hospital in a rickshaw.

AMJAD: We mustn't let our daughter be influenced by these Westernized children. You'll have a shock one day, Banoo, if you catch her kissing a boy. I'll marry her soon.

BANOO: Yes, I think she's ready.

AMJAD: Now you're tiring me. Wait. What about . . . what about what's-his-name?

BANOO: Who is that?

AMJAD: He was in the army with me years ago. He's done well for himself in Hatfield.

BANOO: Hatfield?

AMJAD: Yes, he's got a son called Farouk.

BANOO: Farouk?

AMJAD: We met him. He used to eat sweets all the time.

BANOO: Sweets?

AMJAD: Give me a chance to think. We must make sure Amina has a better life than you've had, eh?

(BANOO goes.)

What's that rich bastard's name? (He shouts.) Banoo! Bring me my writing paper – I'll drop him a line tonight!

RAVI *comes on swinging his suitcase and yelling at the top of his voice.*
He's in the street.

RAVI: Anil! Anil – my brother! It's me – Ravi. Which house is it?
    (*Pause.*) Anil! I've arrived in beautiful England. Did you get
    my letter?

ANIL: (*Opening a window*) What's that noise? Are you insane?

RAVI: Anil, you bloody bastard, my only spiritual brother. It's
    your best friend!

ANIL: I've got no friends. (*He makes to go inside.*)

RAVI: Wait! Don't you recognize me? It's Ravi.

ANIL: It's Ravi. Oh, fuck.

RAVI: Yes. Ravi. We played in the fields together as children,
    Anil. Our arses were wiped by your cousin's relations. We
    had our thread ceremony on the same day. Now I've come
    across the world to stay with you.

ANIL: But what for?

RAVI: Oh welcome me to beautiful England, Anil.

ANIL: (*Under his breath*) Oh, fuck.

RAVI: What?

ANIL: Welcome.
    (*A* WHITE NEIGHBOUR *opens a window.*)

WHITE NEIGHBOUR: Shut down that bleedin' racket for gawd's
    sake.

ANIL: Oh you shut up.

WHITE NEIGHBOUR: Where d'you think you are – Bombay?
    They come over here . . . (*Shuts window.*)

RAVI: Anil, it's taken me two days to find you. Why didn't you
    tell your wife you changed address. You don't realize what a
    relief it is to see your happy face.

ANIL: And you don't realize what a small room I have.

RAVI: I'm coming up.

ANIL: No, no, no, no, wait, no. (ANIL *emerges. They embrace.*)
    Ravi, how did you afford to come here?

RAVI: Let's go in first.

ANIL: Wait. Tell me how you came.

RAVI: My father sold the land.

ANIL: What? Fertile land?

RAVI: Every worm in it, every animal on it.

ANIL: That's typical of your bone-headed father, if I may say so.

RAVI: And the farming equipment, the sheds, the plough. He said I'd soon make it up in England.

ANIL: What? Ravi, you've been badly misinformed, misled and given entirely wrong information by your rotten relations. England's a cemetery.

RAVI: Is it?

ANIL: A crematorium.

RAVI: Anil, but everyone returns to the village rich from England. I've seen it with these eyes.

ANIL: Not any more.

RAVI: I'm tired Anil. I want to lie down. I'm hungry. Let's eat together.

ANIL: Wait. How I like the air in Ealing. It has a calming effect on my soul.

RAVI: Listen. I heard your uncle talking in the village before I left. He was in England once. There was an English girl.

ANIL: Which English girl?

RAVI: He met, he met. She said; 'Are you Indian?' he said, 'Yes, are you English?' She said 'Yes, I'm English.' He said 'You're English are you? Then undress!'

ANIL: It's nothing like that here.

RAVI: No, not at first.

ANIL: Not at all, I assure you my brother. Not at all. English women are stuck-up, cold, racist, common and –

(*An Englishwoman's voice from upstairs.*)

VALERIE: Anil! Anil, what are you doing lovey?

RAVI: Who's that?

ANIL: No idea.

VAL: Come on lovey darling. Your dinner's on.

RAVI: That's funny.

ANIL: You've got to get used to English ways, Ravi.

RAVI: Yes, I want to.

ANIL: They're very particular about us integrating.

RAVI: Are you integrating, Anil?

ANIL: I'm beginning to.

VAL: And you're missing the programme. It's nearly finished.

RAVI: By the way, your wife's looking forward to coming here. She says send the ticket for her and the children as soon as you can. She's been crying, Anil, I know.

VAL: Anil – I'm eating mine. It's your favourite – with peas.

ANIL: Listen, you bastard, I'll break your neck and crush your toes and write to your relatives if you mention my wife in front of my social worker.

RAVI: Social worker?

ANIL: Yes. We all have them here. To teach us English.

RAVI: Really? What a marvellous place England is. I knew it would be.

ANIL: Yes.

RAVI: But will I get a social worker?

(VALERIE *appears*.)

ANIL: You? No. Well . . . No.

RAVI: Can't we go in now, Anil.

VAL: Anil. (*Pause. He freezes.*) Anil.

ANIL: (*Turning*) Valerie! You're there. Drying your hair in the breeze?

VAL: Are you coming in, Anil, or am I locking this door?

ANIL: My flower, give me a minute, I'm just directing Ravi on his way to . . . Manchester.

VAL: (*To* ANIL) Are you coming in?

RAVI: (*Picking up his cases*) Yes, thank you very much.

ANIL: Valerie, Ravi's just popped round to visit me. He's a friend. Of someone.

VAL: Oh yeah. Where you from?

RAVI: Well . . . today?

VAL: No. In general.

RAVI: In general? In general, Anil?

ANIL: Don't ask me.

RAVI: In general I'm from just outside Jullanda.

VAL: Jullanda!

ANIL: Valerie, I think what Ravi's saying – correct me if I'm wrong – is that he's come to deliver a message from my aunt.

RAVI: Yes, I think so.

VAL: What's the message?

RAVI: Er . . . the message. It's right at the bottom of my suitcase.
ANIL: Yes, so we'd better discuss it upstairs.
RAVI: Anil, if it's going to be too much trouble –
ANIL: (*Hopefully*) What trouble, Ravi?
RAVI: I can always sleep on the floor.
ANIL: (*Sarcastically*) Oh, Ravi, no, no, no.
RAVI: I'm so tired I don't mind.
ANIL: Oh no, no, no, no, no.
VAL: Anil, there's only one bed.
ANIL: It's a voluptuous double bed.
VAL: Yes, but I haven't said you could invite half of Jullanda to
       sleep in it.
ANIL: Go upstairs, Ravi, we're just coming.
RAVI: I knew I'd be welcomed.
       (RAVI *goes in.*)
VAL: Anil, I won't put up with this.
ANIL: It's only for one night, Valerie, I promise.
VAL: One night? He's ready for a year, I can see that.
ANIL: I promise you, he'll be gone by tomorrow lunch-time.
VAL: Anil.
ANIL: I know how to get rid of bastards like him. Don't worry.
VAL: I want him gone.
ANIL: Right. But . . .
VAL: But nothing. All right?
       (*She goes in.*)
ANIL: That bastard.

SCENE FIVE

The car park. HAROON *comes on and wanders downstage, waiting for*
AMINA.
ANWAR: Haroon!
       (HAROON *makes to run, as* ANWAR *comes towards him.* ANWAR
       crosses to HAROON.)
HAROON: Anwar.
ANWAR: (*Calling*) Yasmin.
       (*She comes on.*)

Just look at this petrified rabbit we've found nesting in the car park. I told you he'd be here. It's his favourite night-spot.

HAROON: Anwar, I'm tied up right now. I've got some heavy history revision to do and everything. Yasmin, you know I've got exams. It's my A levels.

YASMIN: Have you been doing exams behind Amina's house? Or is that fieldwork for the Duke of Edinburgh's award.

ANWAR: Wait. (*To* HAROON.) Now. I'm not talking as a member of the Asian Youth Movement, but as a friend.

HAROON: Hi, friend.

ANWAR: We haven't seen you in the Youth Movement offices lately.

HAROON: Haven't you?

ANWAR: There's no one to run the magazine now. We raised money for you to start it. We said, 'Go ahead.'

YASMIN: We need to get people organized for what we've got coming. But you've gone on to an altogether higher plane.

HAROON: You do it. Or the others. They're unemployed. The factories are closing down and everything.

ANWAR: But you're the Bruce Lee of writing round here. Novelist too. We're all fond of you. Don't lose touch with your own people.

YASMIN: And don't start thinking white people are interested in you because you had a story in a magazine.

HAROON: I've always fought. They come here. We fry them. We all did that.

YASMIN: Why haven't we seen your girlfriend, Amina? Has she had exams in the supermarket?

HAROON: Ask her yourself. (*Pause.*) Her father keeps her in.

ANWAR: I know that man.

YASMIN: You've had his bloated foot up your arse. I'll go and see her. People are gossiping about you two. If you let it get to her father her whole life will be over. You men don't think about that.

HAROON: (*Going*) Sorry, but I've got to go and use my brain now.

ANWAR: Saturday morning. We're picketing the police station. You with us?

HAROON: Depends on –

ANWAR: Sikh boy found with a carving knife in his leg. Police are claiming it's attempted suicide. Apparently he woke up, saw there was nothing on at the pictures and jammed the knife into himself. Three or four times.

HAROON: Things do get dull in West London.

ANWAR: One more moan. Your father's restaurant. There's this journalist been around.

HAROON: I've seen her. She says she wants to talk to me.

YASMIN: Susan. She's everywhere.

ANWAR: As a treat I took her to your father's restaurant. Thought I'd find out what her game is. She's spellbound. Making notes, making eyes, everything. I'm explaining about the unity of the community here. I glance at the menu. There's a little box at the bottom with a message.

HAROON: His Easter regards to all non-Muslims, I'm sure.

ANWAR: It said, 'We businessmen of the area condemn all those who plan any counter-demonstrations against neo-fascists.'

HAROON: Didn't realize he was so political.

YASMIN: No.

ANWAR: After the meal your father took me aside. He poked me hard in the chest. Told me to stop influencing you. Said he'd break both our backs if you came to the Youth Movement office again.

HAROON: Jesus Christ!

ANWAR: Oh yes. You're going to be a lawyer, he says.

AMINA: (*Off*) Haroon!

ANWAR: Hey. The other rabbit's come to join you in the nest.

HAROON: We come up here for privacy.

ANWAR: Keep away from that journalist anyway.

HAROON: Please and everything.

YASMIN: Yes. If she asks you if you've suffered any racial attacks –

ANWAR: That's her standard opening question.

YASMIN: Say, 'Not until now.'

HAROON: We don't have much time together.

(AMINA *comes on. She's wrapped in layers of clothes wearing a Russian hat with her hair up under it.*)

113

AMINA: Hello.

YASMIN: Hallo, Amina.

HAROON: It's Little Nell.

AMINA: Don't want people recognizing me coming up here.

ANWAR: We've got to go anyway.

AMINA: What's going on?

HAROON: They're interfering with us.

YASMIN: (*To* AMINA) Are your parents well?

HAROON: See.

YASMIN: Are they Amina?

AMINA: They're the same.

ANWAR: We were worried about you, that's all. Sorry if we've interrupted.

YASMIN: You used to drop into the office.

ANWAR: Yes.

YASMIN: It was nice to have you there.

HAROON: You know what her parents are like.

AMINA: They keep me in.

YASMIN: Is it difficult for you at home, Amina?

AMINA: Oh, the neighbours are leaving us alone since Dad got the police in. And the court case is going ahead. But my mother . . .

YASMIN: What?

AMINA: Well, at the moment she's –

HAROON: Amina.

AMINA: It's all right. Let me talk to them. They're friends. I don't know. She hears these noises at night. She goes about from room to room with a torch. Dad shouts at her from the bed till he falls asleep. But it's early morning before she goes to bed.

YASMIN: They're isolated up there. Just up the road, but in a way he's taken you over the borderline. I pity them.

AMINA: You came to the house. My mother told me.

YASMIN: Your father insulted Anwar. He refused to address me. He sent your mother into the kitchen. He said things have quietened down. Is that true?

AMINA: Since he decided to take them to court.

YASMIN: Good. Why don't you come into the office more and help us with the magazine?

114

AMINA: I want to, but I'm not . . . Haroon said you don't need people who can't write.

ANWAR: He's wrong.

YASMIN: He is.

AMINA: Can I come in my dinner hour?

YASMIN: Yes.

AMINA: I will.

ANWAR: That hat.

HAROON: Christ.

AMINA: My hat. (*To* HAROON) Doesn't he look tired? You work too much, Haroon.

ANWAR: He wants to get on.

AMINA: I never see him.

HAROON: I've so much to do. Everyone's down on me.

YASMIN: It's this Tory government that's down on us. That's the issue.

ANWAR: Exactly.

YASMIN: I think the Tories are working towards giving us only guest-worker status here. With no proper rights. That'll bring us into line with some EEC countries. At the same time they're pumping money into the race relations industry. It's probably the only growth area in the country, like hospitals in a war.

ANWAR: It's only to pacify us.

YASMIN: Come to the office, Amina. We'd like to have you around.

AMINA: Yes, okay.

HAROON: Yes, okay. What do you know about it, really? (*To them.*) Can't you leave her mind alone?

AMINA: He's taught me so much, he think's he's my teacher.

YASMIN: I'm sure that being with Haroon is instructive.

HAROON: Come on, Amina, let's go somewhere else.

AMINA: I want to learn. Why shouldn't I? When they threw bricks at the house my father refused to talk about why it was happening.

YASMIN: I had a father like yours.

HAROON: We've all had 'em. You're no freak of nature, Yasmin.

YASMIN: He arranged a marriage for me. I kept refusing. He began to starve himself to death.

HAROON: Jesus.

YASMIN: Yes. He preferred death to being laughed at by his relatives. So eventually I relented. I can still remember his joy – he trembled like a leaf – though he was so weak, his bones poking through his flesh. And the room stank of shit because he hadn't moved from his bed. I know now if he'd died it would have been better for us all. Now as far as they're concerned I'm dead.

AMINA: I didn't know you'd been married.

YASMIN: I don't regard it as a holiday period.

HAROON: What happened then?

YASMIN: What happened?

ANWAR: Haroon.

YASMIN: I'm no longer married to a man. I have understood . . . one or two things about things.

AMINA: I think my father . . .

YASMIN: What Amina? Yes, yes, you must take care.

HAROON: She doesn't want to talk about that.

YASMIN: Don't you?

HAROON: Amina, if you want to yak to these people all night, I'll go to the restaurant – they're short staffed there.

YASMIN: (To HAROON) How's your novel?

HAROON: Why did you say that?

ANWAR: Come on.

AMINA: See you tomorrow.

YASMIN: We'll have a meal. I'll wait for you in the office.

(ANWAR and YASMIN go.)

AMINA: I'd like to talk more to Yasmin. She understands things. She can explain things to me.

HAROON: You're fine as you are.

AMINA: Do you know this car park's not my favourite out of the places we go to. You think a girl likes concrete and car grease against her arse?

HAROON: We've got to talk and everything.

AMINA: No time for that. We'll go in the community workers' shed up by Osterley Park Road.

HAROON: No.

AMINA: Where do you want to go?

116

HAROON: Amina.

AMINA: Eh? What's this then?

HAROON: Amina.

AMINA: (*Pause*) I can see what it is.

HAROON: Amina, please listen.

AMINA: What to? This is me getting the elbow. I could see it
coming. (*Pause.*) Oh yeah. (*Pause.*) Oh you're no bloody
good at it. But I s'pose it's practice for you.

HAROON: Amina.

AMINA: Got to go. My mother's been crying.

HAROON: I'm going away soon. To university and everything.

AMINA: In London. Up the fucking road, you said – up London.

HAROON: It's no good there. Amina, we may as well finish now.
You're . . . you're too attached to me.

AMINA: What?

HAROON: And in October I've got to go miles and miles away. I
didn't think I should leave leaving you to the last minute. We
can become friends before we part.

AMINA: You don't have to go away so far! It's not necessary.

HAROON: I'm cramped here.

AMINA: You are? You are?

HAROON: And you. All of us. Shut in for safety. Strong and solid
now. But stifled here together. Here my brain feels like a
tight ball. The tension. The fighting does that.

AMINA: We call it self-protection here. I s'pose you want white
education. You called it the white lie before. You said they'd
whitewashed history. You'll be playing polo next. What
about the Indian poets? You read them to me.

HAROON: Yeah.

AMINA: And after the riots, when we first went out, I felt – so
happy.

HAROON: We boiled over.

AMINA: Our people are important, you said. We had brooms,
didn't we. We swept away glass where the windows had
gone. We're united here now. We helped unboard shops.
People thanked us. We belong together, you said. We went
in the grass behind the restaurant for the first time. It was
cold. Then it rained. But it was the best day. (*Pause.*) You

know there's rumours they're going to invade us. Burn our shops. We've got to stick together.

HAROON: I'm dispersing. Got to.

AMINA: Little fucker.

HAROON: You know, when we were kids, my brother and I were taken to people's houses. Dressed up and everything. Like being wrapped in brown paper. We just about creaked. In the houses we visit everything's on exhibition: furniture, their wife's hair, their kids, their kids' teeth. You've got to admire everything. They have to admire you, your teeth, hair, shoes. Everything seems to smell of perfume. You can't touch anything. My brother says he has to piss. He's in their hall. I know he's going through their pockets in the hall. I know he's opening their handbags. They're asking me how I'm doing at school. I'm saying I'm doing well. I can hear fivers settling in his pocket. I can hear my father saying, 'Answer them, Haroon, they're our friends.' I can hear myself saying, 'I'm good at English.' That Sunday he steals a car. It's a Jag. I'm lying on the backseat. We're on the bypass. We're doing sixty. We're doing ninety. We're going out to Greenford. I'm completely numb. They're in a house in Greenford. I'm outside. I can hear him and his friends moving across thick carpets, unplugging speakers, lifting down TV sets. I'm looking out. Soon I'm not looking out. In fact I'm running away. I'm away. They're walking down the drive with a spin-dryer. I'm not there. Two men are running towards them. They're arresting them. My father's cursing. My mother's hysterical. I'm locked in my room. I'm studying, I'm protected, I'm the special son, the hope, my brain's burning . . . (*Pause.*) Everyone round here's too busy serving kebabs and learning karate! No one round here knows fuck all about what you want to know about.

AMINA: At least we protect each other here.

HAROON: We've got to engage in the political process. Not just put out fires when they start them. Yasmin and Anwar – they're brave. But they're separatist. I say we've got to get educated. Get educated and get inside things. The worm in the body, Amina.

AMINA: The worm in the body. Sums you up. Especially in bed.

HAROON: It's starting to rain.

AMINA: Journalist came to our house the other day. Coming back
tonight. She's interested in me. I think she's the only white
person I like. I'd like to be friends with her.
(*He kisses her lightly on the cheek. He turns to go.*)
I know men. You know. Asian men. I know them by now.

HAROON: What?

AMINA: I'm an old scrubber now, aren't I. It'll get round about
me. I don't care. I'll be married soon.

HAROON: What's he like?

AMINA: I don't know.

HAROON: Doesn't matter, I s'pose. (*Pause.*) Bye then. (*Pause.*)
It's for the best. Nothing can come of us going on.

AMINA: I want to cry. You know. But I'm not going to let myself.
(*Pause. He runs off. She stands there, takes off her hat. Her hair
falls down.*)

SCENE SIX

SUSAN *at home.* RAVI *is standing there. He's wearing ridiculous
shoes. He has a bloody plaster on his cheek, his trousers are ripped and
dirty and his hair is standing on end.*

RAVI: It took me ages to find your place, Susan. Your directions
completely confused me.

SUSAN: You look as if you've had an accident.

RAVI: Exactly. Fucking exactly.

SUSAN: I'm afraid I've got to go out.

RAVI: Susan, listen. I'm definitely not one of those people who
came here expecting a soft job, a big council house and a
plump social worker.

SUSAN: No, I'm sure.

RAVI: Don't accuse me of taking from the English poor to give to
the Indian poor. I'm ready to work. I've applied for a job in a
restaurant. The owner's a fine man. He was impressed by my
attitude. I could easily go far in the Light of India restaurant.
I'm prepared to take two jobs. Four jobs even.

SUSAN: Yes.

RAVI: But I'm not prepared for . . . I don't want . . . I can't stand
. . . up.

SUSAN: I didn't really expect to see you again, Ravi.

RAVI: No, yes, well, Susan I –

SUSAN: Ravi, you're not trembling?

RAVI: I'm not joking, it's cold. I tell you, I –

SUSAN: Where did you sleep last night?

RAVI: In a cinema.

SUSAN: Where?

RAVI: Soho. Yes, well, no, I've been in bloody trouble, I'm not
joking.

SUSAN: What's happened? You might as well tell a journalist.

RAVI: Yes.

SUSAN: Well?

RAVI: I find my friend, Anil. Go to his flat. His social worker's
there. Valerie. She's right there, sleeping beside us on the
floorboards.

SUSAN: Social worker?

RAVI: She's missed her last bus, you see. Anil and I, we learnt
English together, from nuns. But now . . . it's a cruel
atmosphere. But a good bed. In the morning he goes to work
in the factory. He doesn't say one word to me. The social
worker goes to work. She's a shop assistant. Then I eat
plenty of food. I enjoy myself for the first time in England. I
go to the restaurant, I walk the streets feeling so happy and
determined to do well. I eat a samosa then lie down and wait
for Anil and Valerie to come back. Suddenly the police are
there.

SUSAN: Where, Ravi?

RAVI: At the door downstairs. Anil's discovered I'm not quite
legal here.

SUSAN: I see.

RAVI: Now all the world knows.

SUSAN: Not necessarily.

RAVI: The police ask for me. They have my name.

SUSAN: Anil gave them your name?

RAVI: To get my arse out of his bed. So I say to them, I say, just

one minute, Ravi's upstairs, he's having a bath. I'll fetch
him. I run up. I stand on the window sill. I think of my
mother's face, her greedy face slobbering at the thought of
England. My sisters, sewing, sweating at the thought of me
returning with good things for them. Ahead of me I see the
great housing blocks. I can hear the police coming upstairs. I
jump, I fall and lie there and look at the sky. I think –

SUSAN: What?

RAVI: What am I doing? I feel bad, Susan, bad that I'm tempted
by money here. My father drove the English from India. He
heard Gandhi speak, he was proud. And there I am, hopping
on the leg that isn't busted, away from Ealing.

SUSAN: Your shoes.

RAVI: Under Anil's bed. Believe me. I don't have time.

SUSAN: You can stay here if you want.

RAVI: In this place?

SUSAN: While my flatmate's away. I'll do what I can for you.

RAVI: Thank you very much.

SUSAN: But I'm shifting now. I've got to meet a Pakistani family,
Amjad and Banoo. They've got a beautiful daughter called
Amina.

RAVI: I'll be here then.

SUSAN: So, what are your impressions of England?

RAVI: Apart from what I've said?

SUSAN: If you like.

RAVI: Susan, it's nudity, pure nudity all the time here.
(*He moves towards her.*)

SUSAN: What's the matter?

RAVI: Susan, you are so kind.

SUSAN: Ravi.

RAVI: You're so lovely. Susan, I am Indian.

SUSAN: Yes.

RAVI: You are English, please – undress!

SUSAN: Ravi!

RAVI: I just wanted to touch your lovely round booblas.

SUSAN: Ravi! When I was in India I went to a monastery where
monks could only pass women food with their hands
wrapped in handkerchiefs. An hour later three of them had

put their hands up my skirt. On New Year's Eve I shook a
poor man's hand. An hour later I was in hospital. I do
understand about frustration. But I can't compensate for the
Empire on my own.

RAVI: I've heard so much, Susan.

SUSAN: I'd be interested to hear what you've heard. I'm trying to
make a radio programme at the moment. I want to show
people how things are changing under the skin of England. I
want to chart the pricking of a certain kind of imperial
inflation. I'm from a place called Orpington. It's on the
outskirts of London. It's now a kind of car park. My father
was nothing in Customs and Excise. I managed to get away.
Get a career. It's not easy when all your friends are settling
down with children. I'm not going back. Take off your shoes
if you like.

RAVI: Thank you.

SUSAN: I'll help you if you help me.

RAVI: Have you got a kitchen here?

SUSAN: Through there.

RAVI: Thank you. And my bedroom?

SUSAN: Upstairs on the left.

RAVI: I'll find the bath myself.

SUSAN: You're tired.

RAVI: Yes. But I know that from now on things can only improve.
(*She goes. He takes off his shoes.*)

SCENE SEVEN

Later that night. The house. SUSAN *looking through a photograph
album.* AMJAD *sitting there.*

SUSAN: (*Turning the pages*) They're very nice.

AMJAD: Turn over, Susan. (*She does so.*) My eldest daughter.

SUSAN: (*Sincerely*) She's beautiful.

AMJAD: She's married to an official in the airline, PIA. She has
one son.

SUSAN: I see. And there's your little Amina again.

AMJAD: Yes, laughing like a hyena.

SUSAN: Is she out tonight?

AMJAD: Amina? She's lying down. She'll come in when she's feeling better. You know . . . my wife Banoo likes you.

SUSAN: Does she?

AMJAD: Oh yes. She was very happy when you came here before. She doesn't see many people. Nobody comes to the house.

SUSAN: Does she like England?

AMJAD: Very much.

SUSAN: Do you?

AMJAD: Oh yes.

SUSAN: Can I ask you . . .

AMJAD: Anything. We're pleased to help. Anything!

SUSAN: Have you had any racial trouble?

AMJAD: Nothing.

SUSAN: Really?

AMJAD: We all do. But it's nothing. One or two.

SUSAN: Do you think that kind of thing is increasing?

(BANOO *enters with tea*.)

AMJAD: Banoo come and sit down.

SUSAN: (*To* BANOO) How are you today?

BANOO: Very well, very good. My sewing machine is mended. All day I've worked. (*Pause*.) It's light in here.

AMJAD: (*To* SUSAN) You can ask her anything you want.

SUSAN: It's nice to see you again.

BANOO: And you. (*To him*.) Amjad, shall I pull the curtains?

AMJAD: No. I like the light. I know I'm still alive.

BANOO: (*To* SUSAN) Amjad doesn't mind that everyone looks at us and laughs.

(*Pause*.)

AMJAD: (*Getting up*) You two girls talk together for a few minutes then.

SUSAN: Yes. Thank you. Mr Ali . . .

(*He goes*.)

Banoo.

BANOO: I will talk. I have thought since last time. I have decided. I think you are good. It is poisonous not to speak.

SUSAN: Yes. Have you been out since I was here?

BANOO: I get Amjad's cigarettes. And I go to the airport.

123

SUSAN: Why, Banoo?

BANOO: To think of going home.

SUSAN: You're not happy here?

BANOO: My two daughters are in Pakistan. I want to be with them. I am troubled. Do you understand? (*Pause.*) It's been trouble since we came here. (*Pause.*) Some weeks ago, when I go out, in the street here, the men there expose themselves to me.

SUSAN: They – did that?

BANOO: Yes, I am an old woman. It is the insult.

SUSAN: Yes.

BANOO: For them we are not human, Susan. We are not even –

SUSAN: Sorry, can you just –
(*Pause, while* SUSAN *turns over her tape.*)
Did you tell Amjad about this?

BANOO: I have told no one.

SUSAN: Not even Amina?

BANOO: It would upset her.

SUSAN: Yes.

BANOO: So I hold it inside. I love my own mother still. I told her everything when I was there. But Amina, you can see another life in her eyes, which she doesn't tell.

SUSAN: Are you close to her?

BANOO: I tell you something as a woman to understand.
(*Pause.* SUSAN *realizes the implication and turns off the tape.*)
Thank you. (*Pause.*) I go to Amina's room. She says she is sick. She is not there. I go again, another night. She has gone again. I listen for her. She comes back late each time, like a thief. She does this many times, quietly, leaving open her window. I tell no one. Amjad would . . . yes, he would be angry.

SUSAN: Yes.

BANOO: Whether she is with boys, I don't know. Or with Yasmin, who came here. I don't know. I say nothing to her. She looks at me in the morning. But I say nothing. She has moved far from us. We have lost her, I think. Yes, she must marry soon.

SUSAN: You don't know where she goes?

BANOO: She is roaming there.

SUSAN: It must be worrying for you.

BANOO: It is something I can't understand. We are poor people. Where we come from, education is for the rich. But it has changed her and we can't understand.

SUSAN: But Yasmin is good, I'm sure. She'd look after her.

BANOO: You tell me that and I believe you. I am glad. But Amjad tells me she smokes.

SUSAN: I don't know.

BANOO: She is a girl. (*Pause.*) I will miss Amina here in the house when she is married.

SUSAN: Yes, of course you will . . .

BANOO: No one comes here. She helps me cook and work. I need Amina.

AMJAD: (*Entering*) I will come in now.

BANOO: And he is sick.

AMJAD: Yes, I am sick! But I don't complain. My life is over but I am happy! (*To* SUSAN.) You said before, about my political belief, that thing.

SUSAN: Yes, I did, but –

AMJAD: Put it on. I have inspiration.

(*She turns on the tape recorder.*)

Women don't usually ask such questions, Susan. But I have thought. Tony Benn will be good.

SUSAN: Really?

AMJAD: Oh yes. We like your lords.

SUSAN: You're for the Labour Party then?

AMJAD: We have to be. Yes. I'm for them. But I don't think they're for me.

SUSAN: Banoo, what do you think of that?

AMJAD: Banoo, your face is dropping.

BANOO: My life is misery, I think.

AMJAD: Banoo, Banoo, what's the matter? (*To* SUSAN.) Did you talk well?

SUSAN: We didn't finish, unfortunately.

AMJAD: (*To* BANOO) Did you tell Susan about your village?

BANOO: No, Amjad.

AMJAD: Susan, in my village –

BANOO: Amjad. (*She sobs.*)

AMJAD: Stop it now.

BANOO: I am crying all the time.

AMJAD: All the time.

BANOO: (*To* SUSAN) This is my position.

AMJAD: Wait. The tea has gone cold. Let's have more. (*He shouts.*) Amina – wake up now!

BANOO: You never let me speak, Amjad.

AMJAD: Always.

BANOO: I want to speak.

SUSAN: (*Gently*) And I'd like to hear.

BANOO: This is my position, Susan. I get up. I clean the house. I cook for my husband. Then I work. I sew. He says, 'Don't think. Don't think about anything.' But I am thinking all the time. I am a woman. But I am not afraid. They do their things to us, but I will fight them. I will go out and –

AMJAD: Banoo, you are too excited.

BANOO: I am not afraid. I know what they have done. I know what they want to do. I am afraid for my Amina.

AMJAD: Amina? My Amina is perfect.

BANOO: Amjad, we have made mistakes.

AMJAD: What mistakes?

BANOO: We never realized how English she would become. We can't even write English. She understands life here more than us. We have not helped her here. I feel it, Amjad, when she looks at us, like a little girl. She needs help. Advice. But we are useless. Our ways are no good for her.

AMJAD: Banoo, that's enough.

BANOO: We saved to go back home. But we never had enough money. It was never the right time somehow. Because we wanted more. We became greedy. Now we know we should have gone back long ago. What do we have here?

SUSAN: Well, you have a lovely house.

BANOO: Yes, in the kitchen, one fridge, one oven, one TV there.

AMJAD: Banoo, what are you saying against these things? If you put on the switch and the bulb is gone you are the first to complain.

BANOO: Amjad please, I am saying –

AMJAD: All my life I worked for those things; all your life you wanted them. Now you tell me they are no good! I worked

126

from six in the morning till eleven at night. My back is breaking. Now you say they are nothing.

BANOO: No, Amjad I –

AMJAD: What then?

BANOO: Amjad, calm yourself.

AMJAD: What then, woman?

BANOO: Amjad, you know they haven't made us happy.

AMJAD: (*To* SUSAN) I am happy. You know why? Because I understand the world. I don't expect peace like a child.

BANOO: And our Amina has grown so far from us. We haven't noticed. She has always been a good girl. She has never worn jeans or listened to pop things. But she has grown far away.

AMJAD: Far? She is upstairs! She will come down and kiss her father. We are one family. Did you hear me Banoo?

BANOO: (*To* SUSAN) Amjad no longer hears my voice.
(*Silence.*)
I will go there a few minutes.

SUSAN: Where, Banoo?

BANOO: I will, I think.

AMJAD: Good. You have lost control of yourself.

BANOO: No, Amjad.
(*She goes.*)

SUSAN: I'm sorry. It was my fault.

AMJAD: She's upset. About something. I'll send her on a holiday to Pakistan. (*Pause.*) Your parents don't mind you doing such work?

SUSAN: My parents? Well yes, they do mind. They think it's time I married an architect and had kids.

AMJAD: Exactly. I will make sure my Amina is looked after, by her husband. Our family in Pakistan don't like her working.

SUSAN: Will she marry soon?

AMJAD: Oh yes. We have a few boys in mind. (*Pause.*) I don't want Banoo to be upset. I'll fetch her, shall I?
(*He goes.* SUSAN *adjusts her tape-recorder.*)

AMJAD: (*Off*) Amina! What d'you think you're doing? I thought you were sick and I catch you here. Banoo! You stay there! Come here Amina! Don't walk away from me. I've caught you haven't I!

127

(AMINA *comes in, dressed as for the last scene*.)

AMINA: I think I'm in trouble.

SUSAN: Can I do anything?

AMJAD: (*Just outside, coming in*) Amina!

SUSAN: Is it better that I stay?

AMINA: Yes!

    (AMJAD *comes in*.)

AMJAD: What clothes are you wearing?

AMINA: Papa. These clothes.

AMJAD: (*To* SUSAN) Is this their latest thing now?

SUSAN: Yes.

AMJAD: (*To* AMINA) Have you been out?

AMINA: Papa, I –

AMJAD: Have you? Out in the night?

AMINA: Yes. In the night.

AMJAD: Amina you have deceived us all, the whole family.

AMINA: Papa, I know what I've done.

AMJAD: My heart is paining me tonight and you have done this.

AMINA: Yes, Papa.

SUSAN: Please, I think –

AMJAD: It's all right. (*Pause.*) Susan, just go to Banoo will you for
    one moment. I just want to ask Amina one question before
    she makes tea.

SUSAN: All right.

    (*She goes. He hits* AMINA *across the mouth with the back of his
    hand. He's about to hit her again.*)

AMINA: No, Papa.

    (*The side of her mouth is cut.*)

AMJAD: You're lucky I haven't got strength.

AMINA: Please Papa.

AMJAD: You deserve to be beaten up, Amina.

AMINA: Papa.

AMJAD: Tell me where you've been?

AMINA: To . . . out to see . . . a film.

AMJAD: What the hell for? What film?

AMINA: You don't let me go out Papa. And I like to.

AMJAD: How many times have you done this? (*Pause.*) Three?
    Four? Nine?

128

AMINA: Papa, I want to be a little bit free.

AMJAD: We're finished, the family. Become too English. Your mother's said something right. We should have gone back before. We've done completely wrong things.

AMINA: Papa it's not our fault.

AMJAD: What?

AMINA: There have been things on us. Pushing down.

AMJAD: What things?

AMINA: We all feel threatened since they came to the house. Her mind has gone . . . disturbed. I still have nightmares.

AMJAD: You didn't tell me.

AMINA: Yes and – she's so depressed.

AMJAD: How dare you say these things about Banoo I'll break your bloody face open! You are disturbed. (*Pause.*) Tomorrow I'm speaking again to the family of your future husband, Farouk. They're keen. I don't know why. They're sending him here to meet you.

AMINA: Yes, Papa.

AMJAD: He'll force you to become a good wife.

AMINA: Yes, Papa. (*Pause, in a low voice.*) Those English, they've done all this.

AMJAD: (*In a fury*) What did you say? Repeat what you said. (*Pause.*) No! They haven't done this!

AMINA: Who has?

AMJAD: Mostly the English are good. It's two – maybe five – who do mad things. (*Pause.*) Do you understand me? Do you? (*She says nothing.*)
I can tell you've seen Yasmin. She's your friend.

AMINA: I would be lucky if she was. But I'm too stupid for her.

AMJAD: They are children. I'm worried about you. I can see the way you're heading now. I'll stop it!

AMINA: Yes, Papa.

AMJAD: Now go upstairs. (*Pause.*) Your mouth.

AMINA: What?
(*He indicates.*)
Oh yes.
(*She goes, stops.*) Papa.

AMJAD: What?

AMINA: We can't allow ourselves to be intimidated.

AMJAD: Who taught you these words? You hear them in the supermarket do you? (*Pause.*) You're thinking too much lately.

AMINA: Papa, there's a lot of thinking to be done by all of us. (*She goes quickly.*)

Act Two

SCENE ONE

Music playing as the lights go down: Clapton's 'Give Me Strength'.
SUSAN *comes out into her garden wearing a bikini. She lies in a garden chair, turns off the tape, puts another cassette in the machine, sips her drink.* SUSAN *listening to the tape.*

AMJAD: (*On tape*) Women don't usually ask such questions. But I think Tony Benn will be good.

(*She stops the tape, winds it on.*)

BANOO: (*On tape*) Two daughters in Pakistan. I want to be with them. I'm troubled. Do you understand?

(ANWAR *comes on behind her. He's wearing a tracksuit.*)

ANWAR: You shouldn't leave your side-gate open.

SUSAN: No, I shouldn't.

ANWAR: It's hot today.

SUSAN: Yes.

ANWAR: I've been running.

SUSAN: D'you run a lot, Anwar?

ANWAR: All the movement move a great deal.

SUSAN: Can't you play badminton or something?

ANWAR: We're not keen on playing games.

SUSAN: So you got my message.

(*He says nothing.*)

Well? Are you going to be invaded? Will it be soon? (*Pause.*) So it's only a rumour. I thought so.

ANWAR: It's funny.

SUSAN: What is?

ANWAR: You've been asking everyone I know personal questions. For two weeks I can't turn round in my office without pushing you off a chair. You tell me something. How is Mrs Ali? Or do you call her Banoo? You were seen there.

SUSAN: Is that why you're here?

ANWAR: Can I sit down?

SUSAN: You hate what I'm doing.

ANWAR: Your programme?

SUSAN: And my research.

ANWAR: I've said that, yes. I've said you take our voice. Use our voice. Annexe our cause. Because you like a cause don't you, a good solid cause to tie yourself behind, your brains, energy, all that. Now for a few days you've borrowed our little worry.

SUSAN: I pass on your little worry to anxious people.

ANWAR: No. You change its nature as it passes through your hands. It drips pity. Somehow you say the right things. You talk about our 'problems'. You say we're victims.

SUSAN: Yes.

ANWAR: Of this and that law or boot.

SUSAN: Would you like a drink?

ANWAR: All right.

SUSAN: White wine?

ANWAR: It's the tone of voice you use.

SUSAN: Ice?

ANWAR: The position you have – which reduces us. I suppose these things are always better coming from the patient than the nurse.

SUSAN: I'll get a blank cassette.

ANWAR: (*Taking the drink*) Susan, I know you feel for us.

SUSAN: Don't patronize me.

ANWAR: And when the programme goes out you'll lie in bed reading letters from concerned people. But you never risk anything. Nothing is given up. You believe and believe and believe. You say we have a common cause. But your bed is never any less soft.

SUSAN: What should I do?

ANWAR: For a start don't think you can represent us truly.
(*Pause.*)

SUSAN: There's one thing you can't shift, Anwar.

ANWAR: What?

SUSAN: I do believe it's possible to be honest and accurate about other people's experience. I believe that's important, socially useful, if you like. I genuinely support these values.

ANWAR: Don't you understand? You take our voice. Replace it with your own.

132

SUSAN: Look. I think that a certain kind of gentleness and mildness associated with English life has gone. Even I can remember a kind of tolerance, a certain respect at the heart of things. All that's evaporating. It won't be easy to get back. I trust people like you.

ANWAR: So what?

SUSAN: But I also trust myself. If I thought there was nothing I could do I'd sit at home with a book. The fact that my life isn't lived out under threats and in fear doesn't mean I don't have integrity.

ANWAR: In your world integrity costs nothing. For you integrity is the brand name for an expensive pair of jeans, isn't it?

SUSAN: When are they coming with their knives and petrol bombs? Let's stop it. We'll announce it everywhere. That'll be useful.

ANWAR: It's so lovely here.

SUSAN: What? Yes, it is.

ANWAR: You own it?

SUSAN: No.

ANWAR: I feel like the devil in the garden of Eden. You could be lulled here, your ideas and beliefs becoming a kind of moral exhibitionism, while you turn into the kind of person you hate. You wouldn't even notice it here.

SUSAN: Anyway, why are you here? What do you want?

ANWAR: Talk about Banoo.

SUSAN: All right.

ANWAR: Go on.

SUSAN: I was with the family. They invited me. We were talking.

ANWAR: What about?

SUSAN: She became upset. She seems better now.

ANWAR: Were you asking her personal questions about her private life?

SUSAN: Anwar.

ANWAR: Were you?

SUSAN: Oh fuck off.

ANWAR: Were you? Just answer!

SUSAN: We talked.

ANWAR: That family is in difficulty. They've been through things

133

and they'll go through them again. The father's taking it out on the daughter. Please leave them alone. They don't need you.

SUSAN: I'll continue to communicate the facts about people's lives.

ANWAR: The facts? What will they be? Illiterate village fathers baffled by their kids, downtrodden old women afraid of opening the curtains. White people are our problem and your Government in particular.

SUSAN: Hostile silence is no contribution.

ANWAR: It's not meant to be.

SUSAN: But that's what you believe, isn't it?

ANWAR: Only as far as the wider world is concerned. Not in the community. (*Pause.*) But I thought I'd say something on your tape about this so-called invasion.

SUSAN: Good.

ANWAR: Shall we do it?

SUSAN: Later, I'll finish sunbathing now.

ANWAR: You'll look like a raspberry ripple.

(*He sits beside her and puts his hand on her stomach. He strokes her.*)

SUSAN: I think your arguments are good ones, Anwar.

ANWAR: Do you?

SUSAN: But I'll make the programme anyway.

ANWAR: Of course.

SUSAN: And do it as well as I can. But I'd like you to help me.

(*RAVI has arrived and stands unseen behind them.*)

SUSAN: What did you do before you became a youth leader?

ANWAR: I worked in a shoe polish factory in Slough. We struck for proper wages and they shut it down.

RAVI: I'm not a bit too late am I?

SUSAN: Ravi.

RAVI: I got lost. I get lost everywhere. I feel as if I'm on another planet. Someone spat at me in the street.

SUSAN: What did you do?

RAVI: I ducked my head. These people, they see me, walking on their roads, coming through their towns. They don't like the sight of me. I can understand that. (*Pause.*) Susan, I just can't stay now.

134

SUSAN: I'm taking you to a party this evening.

RAVI: I've got to get back to the restaurant. I just came to tell you. He says I must work tonight.

SUSAN: But we've arranged to go to this party.

RAVI: I know, exactly, I know. But he says I've got to clean the windows, wash the kitchen, all those things – now, tonight. I rushed here in my break.

SUSAN: You just tell him to go and eat a kebab.

RAVI: I just can't, financially, Susan.

ANWAR: Where do you work, Ravi?

RAVI: Light of India restaurant, Union Road.

ANWAR: Haroon's father owns it. A great local philanthropist. Where I took you that day, Susan.

SUSAN: (*To* RAVI) Anwar knows everyone and everything. He's the youth leader.

RAVI: I've jumped in shit up to my neck, Anwar, and now I'm eating it. It's a delicate situation.

ANWAR: Talk about it. What's happened? Trust me, I'm your bloody brother here. I'll help you if I can. What's he paying you?

RAVI: That's it, you see. Bloody less and less. There's no union, nothing. And, well, he's got a hold over me. I can't move.

ANWAR: You're illegal, right?

RAVI: Anwar, as it happens . . . my papers are completely unique. What shall I do? He says either I work or he'll tell the police.

ANWAR: He will, too. They often eat for nothing in his restaurant. No, don't go back there. I'll try and find you a job.

RAVI: Yes, I must send money back. Every night I dream of my mother. I can hear her saying – that terrible bastard, I knew he'd turn out to be useless.

ANWAR: (*To* SUSAN) Take him to the party this evening.

SUSAN: OK.

ANWAR: Now let's make that recording.

SUSAN: Fine. (*To* RAVI) We're going in to talk.

ANWAR: (*To* RAVI) Come and see me in the office tomorrow.

RAVI: Thank you very much.

ANWAR: Where's my drink?

RAVI: (*Shaking his hand*) Thank you very much.

ANWAR: Okay. Okay, I said.

(*As* SUSAN *and* ANWAR *go into the house,* ANWAR *putting his arm round her.*)

SUSAN: Are you ready for trouble?

ANWAR: We have to be.

SUSAN: Don't they know that?

ANWAR: They want a war. It gives them something to do in the evenings.

SUSAN: You do know when it's going to happen, don't you?

ANWAR: I hear things.

(RAVI *stands there and takes off his waiter's bow-tie and jacket.*)

SCENE TWO

The park. AMINA *skates on to the stage.*

AMINA: (*Shouts*) If I disturbed you thinking about your novel don't pant after me like a bloodhound on heat then.

(HAROON *runs on.*)

First hot day this year. You don't hardly notice. You're all inside yourself. The sun.

(*She rolls up the bottom of her salwar kamiz.*)

HAROON: Why not completely undress?

AMINA: D'you know, Haroon, it's taken me two months but I've flushed you out of my system. And I feel like I've swallowed bleach, all right? But I've gone all free and that now, since I last saw you. You'd better get used to it. Must skate down Union Hill this afternoon. It's pretty exciting.

HAROON: What's been happening to you, Amina?

AMINA: I've been recovering from you. Bastard.

HAROON: Recovering? Don't you know what people are saying? You're flying around on those skates; your mother's praying all the time and writing to her relatives. You've been to the pictures with that journalist.

AMINA: It's not illegal is it?

HAROON: Older people in the community are so cruel, the way they gossip. When you're old it's what you do instead of sex.

I've heard your parents are really going through the wringer
and everything.

AMINA: Stick it in your novel.

HAROON: It's hot stuff Amina. It's called *The Empire Strikes
Back*. The last chapter's quite tragic. It's set at your
wedding.

AMINA: No, Haroon. It's not set there and it's not tragic, right?

HAROON: I've heard your future husband's family approve of
you. Is that true? Don't forget to send me an invitation. I'll
get my suit dry-cleaned.

AMINA: Stop it, I said. Stop it.

HAROON: Those marriages are just prostitution. You've got to get
out of it.

AMINA: Why should I?

HAROON: That's why I hate it here and everything. The out-of-
date ways. That ridiculous religion. You've got to say no.

AMINA: I'm not listening to any more of this.
    (*She goes. He stops her.*)

HAROON: Wait. Just wait.

AMINA: What for?

HAROON: Big celebration. Passed my exams.

AMINA: You didn't!

HAROON: Yeah. But you'll be glad when I'm gone. I'll be glad.
There'll be a day soon when everyone's glad. Have you
missed me at all, Amina?

AMINA: Love doesn't stop because you want it to.

HAROON: Not for me either. That's why I've buried myself in
work all this time.

AMINA: You? I've become hard like you now. I've decided to be
pretty icy from now on.
    (*And she tries to pull away from him.*)

HAROON: Amina, when you think of it we'll be dead in fifty years'
time.

AMINA: So?

HAROON: Let's have fun with our bodies while we're still alive.

AMINA: You little turd. After what you've done to me. I cried for
a week.
    (*She tries to hit him. He hits her.*)

HAROON: Jesus, I'm sorry and everything.

AMINA: What am I, a punch-bag now?

HAROON: Sorry. Sorry, I said. I've been hit too. Jesus, Amina, by my old man. And it was Anwar's fault. He came to pressure my old man to give money to keep the Youth Movement offices going. My father was vibrating. He says, 'What I want to see in England is a day when you won't find a single Pakistani on the shop-floor. You never see Jews in overalls. We've got to develop our businesses, our power. You punks disrupt everything.'

AMINA: Anwar's not a punk.

HAROON: Amina, I said to the old man, 'Why don't you let them join a union? Make a gesture towards the defence fund!' Amina, he came at me – and he punched me in the teeth. (*Pause.*) I mean it, you can turn to me if you need someone now. I'll help you if I can and everything.

AMINA: Don't bother to exert yourself. I've got someone.

HAROON: That Susan?

AMINA: No.

HAROON: Who? You haven't. Who?

AMINA: Myself. I told you. I've gone all free.

HAROON: Keep away from that Susan then. Anwar's handling her. He's got her tied up in ideological knots.

AMINA: But why? She's kind.

HAROON: Those prying white people. What do they want to understand about us? They've got it coming, that's all they need to know. Someone's going to burn out their eyes for all they've done round the world to people.

(SUSAN *come on.*)

SUSAN: Amina.

AMINA: Hallo.

SUSAN: (*To* HAROON) I've just seen your dad.

HAROON: What?

SUSAN: He's driving round in a Range Rover. He stopped me to ask if I'd seen you.

HAROON: Oh no.

SUSAN: It's busy in the restaurant. He wants you there.

HAROON: Oh Jesus!

138

SUSAN: He's so happy now you've passed your exams. But he said it's time you did some real work instead of hanging round with those revolutionaries. I told him not to worry, Haroon's not disaffected. He's just affected.

HAROON: He'll kill me, Amina.

(*He rushes off.*)

SUSAN: Has he upset you?

AMINA: Not today.

SUSAN: Your face.

AMINA: What about it?

SUSAN: You're very beautiful. Are you on the picket tonight?

AMINA: Are they having one?

SUSAN: I thought you knew about it.

AMINA: Oh picket. Picket. Thought you said picnic. Picnic. It'll be bizarre.

SUSAN: Why?

AMINA: I can't explain. (*Pause.*) D'you know, the sun makes no difference to my parents. I think I'd kill myself if I didn't think it would kill them.

SUSAN: I don't believe you'd do that.

AMINA: Why not? Anyone could have my life.

SUSAN: How?

AMINA: Yes, any bastard could be more constructive, couldn't they. Make more of it than me. All the things people've done to my parents. And what have I done to help them? The council have done more. I can't let them down now.

SUSAN: Is your father still imitating a silent Buddha?

AMINA: He doesn't talk to anyone. He doesn't look at our faces. He just sits there like stone, all day, all night.

SUSAN: Is your mother still praying all the time?

AMINA: When she's not telling me how happy I'll be when I'm married. (*Sarcastic.*) I can't wait to have a family of my own. How's your work?

SUSAN: I can't get it out of my mind. All the people I've spoken to have been beaten or burnt or abused at some time. You speak to them, they say they like England, it is democratic, or just, or good. And then say what's been done to them here. Such viciousness in England. No wonder people here

139

don't like to leave the area. No wonder Anwar's suspicious. Amina, I will try and make a good programme. People don't know what it's like in their own country.

AMINA: Who have you seen?

SUSAN: I was at a house across the park with a Gujarati boy. He was shot with an airgun.

AMINA: In the riot two years ago?

SUSAN: No, outside Sainsbury's. In the back of the head.

AMINA: Oh him.

SUSAN: You know him? I suppose he's a local martyr.

AMINA: Ol' headache? Not likely. He drove a car at Anwar once. He called the Youth Front a bunch of communists. Last week he joined us. He went up to Yasmin to shake hands and she said, 'There's nothing like a bullet in the brain to raise consciousness.' He went white.

SUSAN: And this morning, Amina, I went back to see a woman from Bangladesh. Her son was found naked in the garden with Fascist symbols carved into his stomach and legs. The police say he was mugged. How do you live with all this?

AMINA: Ask Yasmin.

SUSAN: I will.

AMINA: D'you know, Susan, sometimes you think, 'I don't care if that bloke got tattooed with penknives. Don't care if they try to get us this week. Or next week.' You can't cure things can you? All you want is your lover to love you. That's the most important thing. But that's so cruel. See you.

(*She walks away.*)

SUSAN: Your skates.

AMINA: Chuck them in the boot of your car till tomorrow. They're hot.

SUSAN: What?

AMINA: Nicked from work. I've got it coming, haven't I.

(YASMIN *enters.*)

YASMIN: You're out here too.

AMINA: I was just coming to see you.

YASMIN: (*To* SUSAN) How are you getting on?

SUSAN: Very well. People are eager to talk.

YASMIN: There is much to be said.

SUSAN: Yes there is. But you won't talk to me.

YASMIN: Why should I? Anwar and I agree, in the main. And I believe you two are communicating . . . quite often.

SUSAN: I want to ask you about yourself.

YASMIN: I have had an unhappy life. Yes, white people would like an exhibition of my misery. But before I go emotionally nude for them, tell them to look at their own history.

SUSAN: I'll pass on your message.

YASMIN: Yes, do that.

(*They look at each other, then laugh.*)

SUSAN: I'm tired. I'm going home. Bye, Amina.

(*She goes.*)

AMINA: I like Susan. You're so hard on her.

YASMIN: She's great fun.

AMINA: What?

YASMIN: Oh I've got no idea. She means well, yes.

AMINA: Are you sad today?

YASMIN: No, just thinking how to control an office full of angry, ignorant boys. They smoke and sweat and boil over. They talk of petrol bombs, they explain how to saw off a shotgun. I tell them to learn how to read and write. But they hate anything that takes longer than a night to achieve.
Apparently they intend to do something about the stabbing. They're definitely not prepared to rely on either the police or prayer. (*Pause.*) Oh, I'm tired. I work so hard. And I can feel myself becoming too austere. Yes. When people do weak things they look guiltily at me. Or avoid me. Anwar.

AMINA: I see.

YASMIN: He is worried that weakness is capitulation. Stupid. I think I should fuck more.

AMINA: Yes.

YASMIN: What's Haroon like? No. Sorry.

AMINA: Can I say something?

YASMIN: If it's funny (*Pause.*) No. What is it?

AMINA: Suppose . . . suppose you're in this situation. And you have to decide. You just have to. And if you did one thing you'd hurt people you love and nothing could be the same again. But if you did the other thing, what they want, you'd hurt yourself.

YASMIN: How badly?

AMINA: Badly. Badly.

YASMIN: I won't decide things for you. You're too intelligent.

AMINA: Yasmin, please.

YASMIN: No.

AMINA: Yes, you're right. I've decided already. I won't . . .

YASMIN: What?

AMINA: I'm not going to resist.

YASMIN: I see.

AMINA: I'll marry him.

YASMIN: There'd be just too much tearing of tissue all round, you mean.

AMINA: My father.

YASMIN: Him?

AMINA: Yes.

YASMIN: I've told you my own marriage wasn't a frolic.

AMINA: Yasmin, can't you understand? I can't be tough like you. I just can't be. I can't. Sorry, I can't. I'm too frightened.

YASMIN: Well.

AMINA: Yasmin, tell me what to do.

YASMIN: Go through with it then. For them.

AMINA: It would be evil to defy them. You can't see that can you? What would I do with my freedom anyway. I don't think I can do good like you.

YASMIN: Your father is too sick to defy.

AMINA: Yes, yes.

YASMIN: Go through it then. Then come out of it.

AMINA: Could I?

YASMIN: Maybe. In time.

AMINA: I make you feel sick, I'm so weak. Don't you turn against me.

YASMIN: I'd never do that.

AMINA: You have already.

YASMIN: Only a bit.

AMINA: Oh, and this is silly. I'm not a virgin and I'm afraid my husband will complain to my father about it.

YASMIN: Oh that. I tell you, you just scream at the right moment, that's an orgasm in itself for men. And beat their backs with your fists, tear their skin. When they complain say your passion overcame everything. And have no brats.

AMINA: D'you know, the first time I met my future husband, Farouk, he picked his nose and wiped it on his tie.

YASMIN: What kind of tie was it?

AMINA: A big fish one. So bright he had to wear dark glasses.

YASMIN: Do you like this weather?

AMINA: I love it, yes.

YASMIN: Do you? I always think the English talk too much about that stuff.

SCENE THREE

HAROON *in the office of the Youth Movement, writing in a notebook.*
SUSAN *comes on, carrying a camera.*

SUSAN: What time's everyone coming?

HAROON: Now.

SUSAN: I've got something for Amina.

HAROON: She's meeting her future husband tonight.

SUSAN: Oh dear. You're on this picket are you?

HAROON: Yes. I'm the spearhead.

SUSAN: Picketing your own father's restaurant. Shitting on your own doorstep.

HAROON: To be honest, it's an Oedipal nightmare isn't it?

SUSAN: Are you really going to take part?

HAROON: I'm not answering questions. I won't be fodder for the media. Right. (*Pause.*) How's it going?

SUSAN: I've got about fifteen interviews down. I never realized it would all be so violent.

HAROON: No, well.

SUSAN: This family. They had their furniture sawn up. They went out to do some shopping . . .

HAROON: Don't draw me a picture, it's only news to you.

SUSAN: I thought you were a novelist, interested in these things.

HAROON: These kinds of incidents and things wind you up. I'm not too keen on the English at the moment. They're not

143

exactly my favourite race of all time.

SUSAN: You don't like your own people much.

HAROON: No.

SUSAN: Who do you like then?

HAROON: I read a lot. You look the type who goes to dinner parties.

SUSAN: Do I?

HAROON: Yeah, I can see you with clever people who like avocado vinaigrette. They'd hate me. I'd turn their guts right over.

SUSAN: They'd rather take you up, I think.

HAROON: Yeah, but I'd hate them, you see. That's my main problem. I'm fascinating, but spiky as hell.

SUSAN: They'd like that.

HAROON: They'd like everything, these people. They've obviously got no discrimination at all. I wonder why I can't wait to be invited round.

SUSAN: It's because you're young and over-excitable. Whereas to me the life here seems vigorous and rich. I wish I could be part of it.

HAROON: You?

SUSAN: Yes. I expect my life to become easier. I mean, my career could become like playing a game. Anwar's right, you know the moves and you make them. You see, I haven't failed. I'm not a dental nurse as my mother wanted. But where have I got? Most of the work I've done has meant little to me. It's all earnest and done well. But it doesn't mean much. Whereas you've got a cause, a direction.

HAROON: Listen, I passed my exams. Nothing here matters to me now. Fuck you all. The future's waiting for me.

(*Enter* ANWAR, YASMIN *and* RAVI *carrying placards and pens.*)

ANWAR: Come on, let's get on with it.

YASMIN: We're meeting the others there?

ANWAR: Yes, I've spoken to them already.

YASMIN: I spotted a guy from the local paper.

ANWAR: We'll give him something to write about then.

(AMINA *runs on.*)

AMINA: Sorry if I'm late.

YASMIN: How did you get out of the house?

144

AMINA: Staff training, sudden decision by the manager.

YASMIN: That's risky isn't it?

AMINA: It's practically my last night of freedom. If they hadn't let me go, I'd have gone through the window.

RAVI: Anyone lend me a fiver?

ANWAR: Amina, give us a hand with this. Then I'll tell you what we're going to do.

RAVI: Please, I'm in a bit of financial shit at the moment.

ANWAR: (*Offering pen*) Haroon.

HAROON: No. (*He walks away.*)

YASMIN: Did you see your future husband then? Where did he wipe his nose this time – on your sleeve?

AMINA: He's coming to meet me tonight.

YASMIN: I'll give him a handkerchief as a wedding present.

AMINA: Yasmin, I don't feel like joking about it.

YASMIN: All right. Asian people are so fatalistic. That's our problem.

RAVI: You haven't got a spare pound have you Susan? My wallet was stolen in a takeaway by a bastard Sikhara. You can't trust them.

SUSAN: Oh Ravi, I can't keep shelling out on you.

RAVI: I understand your point of view, Susan.

YASMIN: We think that nothing under the sun can be changed.

ANWAR: Amina, why don't you go and ring Raj. Tell him we'll meet him and the others by the dairy.

AMINA: Right. (*She goes.*)

RAVI: Haroon, you haven't got fifty pence have you?

HAROON: You owe me money from that card game we played with the other waiters.

YASMIN: The older members of the community don't like this kind of thing.

ANWAR: But we can't worry about that.

HAROON: Ravi, you're still alive and healthy anyway.

RAVI: Yes I am. But don't tell your father.

ANWAR: Their wealth never reaches us, does it?

YASMIN: That's true.

HAROON: The last time I saw you, you dropped a tandoori chicken in someone's lap.

RAVI: Don't remind me. Your father treated me like a slave in that smart restaurant of his. I've been pretty sick. One of the bastard Bengali waiters put laxative in my food because he wanted my job for his brother. I'm telling you Haroon, in confidence, I'm practically starving.

HAROON: Here. (*He gives him money.*)

SUSAN: Haroon, you must write to Ravi's parents for him.

HAROON: OK.

RAVI: Yes. Tell them how well I'm doing. And tell them I'm changing address soon.

HAROON: Where to?

RAVI: Clapham Common. I've heard the grass is soft there.

SUSAN: My flat-mate has come back. Ravi has had to move.

ANWAR: Susan, come and give us a hand. You're a writer.

RAVI: Susan, please tell Anwar I'm still waiting for him to get me that job in the biscuit factory.

SUSAN: Don't pressure him all the time. (*She goes over.*)

ANWAR: Write this on the card.

RAVI: You don't know any women do you?

HAROON: I used to know one.

SUSAN: You know it'll be all over the local papers, this picket.

RAVI: In the letter you must say there's been a delay in me moving into the flat I've bought in Muswell Hill.

HAROON: You've told your parents you've bought a flat in Muswell Hill?

RAVI: Haroon, they're sitting in India expecting me to succeed. I can't tell them I caught crabs from a prostitute and sleep in a field. They don't expect me to be doing that in a country that had the world's greatest empire. You can do that in Bombay.

HAROON: You should be in Dubai.

RAVI: I know. Where is it exactly? How's your brother?

AMINA: (*Returning*) They'll meet us there, Raj says.

ANWAR: Good.

HAROON: I feel sorry for Amina.

RAVI: Why?

HAROON: Look at her. She's a better person than any of us here.

YASMIN: Amina, use red for that.

HAROON: She loathes me now. I had to wean her off me.

ANWAR: Did Raj say how many of them there'd be.

AMINA: Five or six, I think.

HAROON: Look at her life. What chance has she got of getting free?

ANWAR: We'd better move then.

HAROON: My brother? They talked about him being in prison, did they, the other waiters?

RAVI: Oh yes.

HAROON: My father thinks they talk about nothing else. What shall I write?

SUSAN: (*To* YASMIN) Do you know Haroon's father?

YASMIN: Do I know that bastard? He only employs immigrants. They have stronger arms, he says, and they eat less. At the same time half the Youth Movement are unemployed. It's us that's keeping them out of trouble and he calls us disrupters. Isn't that true. Haroon?

HAROON: Yasmin, please and everything. Muswell Hill, did you say?

RAVI: Make it Hampstead.

YASMIN: (*To* SUSAN) The day of the Southall riot.

SUSAN: (*Unobtrusively turning on her tape recorder*) Yes, what happened?

YASMIN: We're on the street. Haroon's mother's with us. We run back to their house. The police are behind us. We try to get in. Haroon's father has pushed the kitchen table against the door. His wife ended up with ten stitches in her head. There's no future for people like Haroon's father.

HAROON: Yasmin. In Bangladesh you'd have starved to death by now.

YASMIN: Maybe.

HAROON: Here – you're on a diet.

YASMIN: Are you trying to say something, Haroon?

HAROON: Yes. You come to this country and everything. You picket my father. His family in Pakistan were killed in the floods. For twenty years he's worked. You try and destroy him. Your own people.

YASMIN: He's no Gandhi is he?

ANWAR: Ravi will tell you he's not.

147

RAVI: Well, he's not actually.

AMINA: He's done well in England. We all want that, Yasmin.

RAVI: I do.

ANWAR: He's only done well because other people have sweated. Mainly into the food I think.

YASMIN: Haroon, if this is how you feel, I'm surprised you decided to come tonight at all.

AMINA: Why shouldn't he come, Yasmin?

HAROON: Yes, why say that Yasmin?

YASMIN: I thought you might prefer it at home, writing your novel. It's full of feeling, I've heard. It's subtle with suffering. Whose suffering, Haroon?

HAROON: Yasmin, literature's right above your head.

YASMIN: Alternatively, I thought you might be trying to destroy Amina this evening.

HAROON: What do you mean?

ANWAR: Yasmin, sit down.

AMINA: Please stop it.

HAROON: Wait. What do you mean. Yasmin?

YASMIN: We know what you've been saying, in the pool hall, in the pinball arcade and those places you go. (*To* AMINA.) It's the truth, sister, believe me.

AMINA: I don't know anything about this.

HAROON: Shut up.

ANWAR: Haroon, you're making things worse for yourself.

HAROON: I'm sick of you people going on at me like this. No wonder I can't wait to leave.

YASMIN: The truth about yourself makes you cringe.

HAROON: The worst thing about being on the left is the other people you've got on your side.

YASMIN: We know you and what you want, what you think you're leaving for. You want to be a lawyer, eh? Because you believe in slow progress, using existing machinery. But we can't wait for the race relations board to prosecute someone. People are being burnt to death. You're no different to your father.

HAROON: Yasmin, you're not the only moral person round here! (*He pushes her to the ground.*)

148

ANWAR: Cut it out!

SUSAN: Haroon, calm down.

ANWAR: It's none of your business.

AMINA: He's always hitting people. He's a screwball.

YASMIN: It's people like you and your repulsive father who hold
us back.

HAROON: How?

YASMIN: How? You haven't noticed? By exploiting their own
people. By not facing the issues. By pretending they've
found a safe place here. By thinking that the fact they've
made money gives us all position and respect in some way.
What are we really all up against? Passport raids,
harassment, interrogation, repatriation by intimidation,
detention centres at Heathrow Airport. Haroon, you're in a
bad way.

AMINA: He is, so leave him.

ANWAR: Let her finish.

YASMIN: I understand what you're going through, because it's
happened to me. To many of us. You've taken all the
conflicts inside yourself. But you can't live like that, as if race
and contempt and all that was some kind of personal
problem you can work through on your own. It'll tear you
apart in the end. No, we've got to organize and retaliate.

HAROON: I want to live a normal life. I suppose.

YASMIN: You can't.

HAROON: We're developing a siege mentality and everything. It's
distorting us.

YASMIN: It's strengthening us. We know who we are.
(*Pause.*)

ANWAR: Right. Let's get on with this thing then. Yasmin, you'd
better tell Raj we don't want anything smashed.

YASMIN: Right.

ANWAR: We just want to kill his business for a night.

YASMIN: We'll certainly do that.

SUSAN: Can I ask something?

ANWAR: If it causes less chaos than your last little question.

SUSAN: Is killing his business for a night all you want to achieve
with this picket?

ANWAR: No. There's a council meeting tonight. And they often
go there to eat. And it's a well-known place; white people
come from miles around.

SUSAN: Yes.

ANWAR: We'll let them know what bugs there are behind the
flocked wallpaper. It's only a gesture, but not a pointless
one.

HAROON: Anwar, it is pointless. I'm telling you, we've got to be
properly influential in this country. Join parties, sit on
committees, work for papers.

YASMIN: They just dilute you. Absorb your anger. We've got a
base here.

HAROON: Narrow. You're narrow people.

ANWAR: We've got to do things here, now! Protect these people
here, now. You're too theoretical.

YASMIN: Go and join the Labour Party. Go and collaborate with
that stagnant racist organization.

HAROON: You people, you come from villages, you've still got
village mentalities, and English people will always treat you
like fucking villagers.

(*He goes off in a fury.*)

ANWAR: Let's shift.

(YASMIN *and* RAVI *go.*)

ANWAR: (*To* SUSAN) Give me the tape you just made.

SUSAN: (*Gives him tape*) Are you coming to dinner on Thursday?

ANWAR: I shouldn't really.

SUSAN: You're welcome, you know that. What about Saturday?

ANWAR: Look. Maybe. Probably. I'll call you.

SUSAN: You won't though.

ANWAR: Saturdays we patrol the area for trouble. What will they
say if they find out I'm lying on a waterbed with a noseful of
coke.

SUSAN: They'll say they all want some of it.

(ANWAR *holds her.* YASMIN *comes on.*)

YASMIN: Anwar.

ANWAR: Yasmin, just coming.

YASMIN: All right.

SUSAN: Sorry, it's my fault.

ANWAR: No.

YASMIN: Anwar.

(YASMIN *and* ANWAR *go*.)

AMINA: Aren't you on the picnic?

SUSAN: I'm waiting for you.

AMINA: I'm getting home.

SUSAN: I see. Here. Here's some books. (*She opens a bag*.)

AMINA: Books?

SUSAN: That I thought you might like to read. Different things.

AMINA: Literature. Did you bring them especially?

SUSAN: Yes.

AMINA: Well, I don't read much. Haroon reads a bit.

SUSAN: It shows. OK?

AMINA: Thanks, Sue.

SUSAN: It's a pleasure.

AMINA: Don't worry, I won't give them to Oxfam.

SUSAN: No, don't do that. And don't get married.

AMINA: What?

SUSAN: Please be careful.

AMINA: I've got to go.

(RAVI *runs on*.)

RAVI: Amina, Haroon's just, well, he's chucked a chair through
his father's restaurant window.

AMINA: Typical.

RAVI: The customers are covered in glass.

(SUSAN *runs off*.)

Yasmin's furious. She says it's personal and not political. Or
is it political and not personal?

AMINA: Sorry, Ravi, I've got to go home.

(AMINA *goes*. RAVI *sits down at the table. He puts his feet up. A
policeman comes on*.)

BILL: Excuse me, sir.

RAVI: (*Jumping up*) Yes?

BILL: I'm looking for someone called Mr Ravi.

RAVI: Ravi, Ravi, Ravi.

BILL: Yes. Know him?

RAVI: Funny you should ask me that.

BILL: Is it, sir?

151

RAVI: He's – he's just chucked a chair through a window.

BILL: He has, sir?

RAVI: Over there. Come on, I'll show you. I'll point him out to you. Then I must be off. I'm leaving for Dubai tonight.

BILL: Dubai, sir?

(*They go off.*)

SCENE FOUR

FAROUK *and* AMJAD *sitting on the sofa,* BANOO *in the armchair. Tray of tea on the coffee table.*

AMJAD: Farouk, would you like some more tea?

FAROUK: No, no, no. Thank you.

AMJAD: This is a quiet area. We retired here especially.

FAROUK: But on my way here I saw a disturbance outside a restaurant. I know there's been unrest in Asian areas recently. Some of our young people are uncontrollable.

BANOO: Yes, their parents can't control them.

AMJAD: They don't feel at home here. It is very sad.

BANOO: Amina is usually punctual.

AMJAD: What? (*To* FAROUK.) Yes, she's a wonderful girl, as your father knows. But she's shy.

BANOO: Oh yes, she's very quiet and –

AMJAD: Banoo. (*To* FAROUK.) So you've just come back from the factory?

FAROUK: Yes, I came straight here.

AMJAD: And how is everything there? You're expanding the business, I hear.

FAROUK: We are working very hard. We've received a big order.

AMJAD: Yes, your father told me. Oh yes, and he has told me what a great asset you are to him.

FAROUK: No, no, no.

AMJAD: Oh yes. We have gone into everything. He's been here several times recently.

BANOO: We should be so happy to have you as our Amina's husband.

AMJAD: I have always wanted a son like you. He says you want to open these boutiques, eh?

152

FAROUK: Yes I do.

AMJAD: That shows initiative.

FAROUK: And it is difficult to find good labour in the rag trade these days.

AMJAD: The English just don't want to work. They want us to work.

FAROUK: We don't employ English.

AMJAD: Very wise, Farouk. Give your own people a chance.

FAROUK: Yes. Women at home. They like something to do.

BANOO: Yes, I have a little job –

AMJAD: Banoo. (*To* FAROUK.) Our Amina was born here, as you know. But she's Pakistani through and through. She hasn't taken up Western ways like some of our girls. You see them in jeans. That's the big advantage with our Amina.

FAROUK: It's very good, I must say.

AMJAD: She's only interested in children.

FAROUK: I long to have a son.

AMJAD: Farouk, please, give me a grandson before I die.

FAROUK: It depends how old you are, Mr Ali.

(*They laugh.*)

No, I must be established in business first.

AMJAD: That's a major priority.

(AMINA *comes in, carrying the books.*)

Amina, my love.

BANOO: There's someone here to see you.

FAROUK: Hallo Amina.

AMINA: Hallo Farouk. (*Silence.*) Shall I make more tea?

BANOO: No, let me.

AMJAD: Good, Banoo.

BANOO: Yes, and you come and help me Amjad.

AMJAD: Me? Oh, yes, yes.

(*They go.*)

FAROUK: Do you like that job, Amina?

AMINA: It's all right.

FAROUK: Do you like Hammersmith?

AMINA: Pardon?

FAROUK: I've got a house there, which my father bought me.

AMINA: I've never been there.

153

FAROUK: It's clean and respectable at least. But most of England's a miserable place.

AMINA: It's made my parents miserable.

FAROUK: I think we'll go to America or Canada eventually.

AMINA: I'd be glad to leave my job in the supermarket.

FAROUK: Oh yes, straight away. You know I don't like women to work.

AMINA: I have to.

FAROUK: Yes, but isn't there something degrading about it?

AMINA: And I help my mother. She works.

FAROUK: What does she do?

AMINA: She's a homeworker.

FAROUK: I didn't know that. And we were just talking about it. She works here?

AMINA: And they pay her so little.

FAROUK: I see. What books are these?

AMINA: Someone gave them to me.

FAROUK: All the time I'm working, you know. I'm determined to do well. I'll enjoy life later. I'll open discos – things like that. Expand. Amina, there's so much to do. (*Pause*.) When do you read these things?

AMINA: In bed, Farouk.

FAROUK: In bed? Show me.

(*She gives him the books*.)

I don't recognize any of the titles. *Crime and Punishment*. Are they detective stories?

AMINA: I like to read a whole variety of things. Some of them are quite deep.

FAROUK: You're very confident for a girl. Do people say you're shy?

AMINA: I don't know.

FAROUK: You don't know? I don't think you're shy. That's another wrong thing your father said.

AMINA: My father doesn't lie.

FAROUK: He exaggerates, eh? Of course he does. I don't mind. All Pakistanis do. Even me! I can see you're much more Western than he said. But I am Western. We're the new modern kind of Pakistani. And I like a challenge.

AMINA: Do you see me as that, Farouk?

FAROUK: I will be honest. I am easily bored with those sweet docile types who live here as if they're back home in their village. They live in an unreal world. They don't know how to give their husbands proper support. So you see we are a progressive family. (*Pause.*) Perhaps you and I will go to the cinema with my sisters.

AMINA: I'll speak to my father.

FAROUK: Yes. (*Rising.*) And I will ring next week.

AMINA: (*Suddenly*) Farouk.

FAROUK: Yes? (*Pause.*) What is it?

AMINA: You will have to make allowances for me. I was born and brought up here.

FAROUK: Of course. I have great experience of these things!

(*They look at each other.* BANOO *and* AMJAD *enter.*)

AMJAD: Farouk.

FAROUK: Actually I think I must be going.

AMJAD: Stay, stay a few minutes more. Doesn't your father want to know anything more?

FAROUK: I'm very satisfied. Things seem to be getting sorted out.

AMJAD: You're satisfied?

FAROUK: (*Looking at* AMINA) Almost.

BANOO: Oh we're so happy.

AMJAD: Yes, yes we are.

FAROUK: Well, goodbye.

AMJAD: Goodbye Farouk.

FAROUK: Amina.

AMINA: Farouk.

(FAROUK *goes.*)

AMJAD: What a lucky girl you are, Amina. I told you I'd take care of it.

BANOO: Oh yes. He's very handsome.

AMJAD: Of course.

BANOO: He looks like an Indian film star.

AMJAD: Their family is highly respected and wealthy. Banoo, you don't realize how lucky we've been.

BANOO: I do realize it, Amjad.

AMJAD: You know, I don't feel well.

BANOO: Amjad.

AMJAD: It's the happiness and excitement I think.

BANOO: You rest then.

AMJAD: Yes.

BANOO: Sit back.

(*He sits there with his hand over his face.*)

BANOO: (*To* AMINA) What do you think of Farouk?

AMINA: He is everything a father could want.

BANOO: So you don't like him at all.

AMINA: I'm supposed to grow to like him.

BANOO: He's the first boy you've seen, Amina. Perhaps Papa will
find you someone else. Don't be afraid of saying no. You
don't have to go for the first boy who comes here.

AMJAD: (*Depressed and feeling ill*) Why are you talking against me,
Banoo?

BANOO: Amjad, rest, rest.

AMJAD: How can I?

AMINA: Is Papa all right?

BANOO: (*Leading her away.*) I was up all night, tending to him.
He said he was dying. And he became frightened like a child.
He began to blame us. He became so bitter against life and
against us. I've never seen him like that.

AMINA: Oh poor Papa.

BANOO: So we must not upset him.

AMJAD: Banoo.

BANOO: What is it?

AMJAD: Say you like the boy.

BANOO: You know I do.

AMJAD: Say it in a convincing way.

BANOO: I like him.

AMINA: (*Going to him*) I like him Papa.

AMJAD: I knew you would. You're a lovely girl.

BANOO: Let me get your pills and some water (*She goes.*)

AMJAD: Amina, today I have secured your future. You'll be
happy, I know you will. Ever since you were a sweet little
girl I've only wanted your happiness. Recently . . . you see
I've been afraid you might get involved in political,
dangerous things. If you live in England and let them turn

156

you anti-English there will never be a moment's peace. Do you understand?

AMINA: Yes.

AMJAD: You will always be in opposition.

(BANOO *comes in.*)

BANOO: Take these Amjad. Then you must go upstairs to bed.

AMJAD: No. I want the doctor.

BANOO: Are you sure?

AMJAD: Do what I say. (*To* AMINA.) Go to the phone box. I understand nothing about my family but I understand when I'm dying.

BANOO: You've said this before, and the pain has passed.

AMJAD: I hope I live long enough to say it again, and long enough to hear you both mock me for it. Now go.

(AMINA *goes.*)

BANOO: (*Takes his hand*) Don't talk too much now.

AMJAD: They will come in a minute. You see how good things are here. In Pakistan if you send for an ambulance there is a day's delay – then a hearse arrives.

BANOO: Quiet, quiet.

AMJAD: Yes, yes. Don't leave me Banoo.

(*They sit there. Fade.*)

SCENE FIVE

The office of the Youth Front. HAROON *comes on, carrying his suitcase.*

HAROON: Amina! Amina! Come and say goodbye to me properly before everyone else arrives.

(*Pause.* AMINA *comes on, carrying papers and a stapler. She's had her hair cut short. She's wearing English clothes for the first time: skirt and T-shirt.*)

Let's part on good terms. Please, Amina.

AMINA: Goodbye, Haroon. What time's your train?

HAROON: Amina, why is it when it comes to the new life one never wants to go? Why can't you say goodbye properly?

AMINA: Can't you see I'm doing this.

157

HAROON: You're like a social worker or something.

AMINA: I spent a month in Pakistan for my father's funeral.

HAROON: I know that.

AMINA: My mother stayed there. I belong here. There's work to be done. To make England habitable.

HAROON: It never will be so we might as well part properly.

AMINA: Go away.

(YASMIN *enters*.)

What's happening, Yasmin?

YASMIN: I've spoken to the police again. They say the Fascist meeting must go ahead. We won't get within 500 yards of the church hall. They're driving into town from various directions. Some of us should try to stop them. I'll see to that. (*To* HAROON.) Or will you do it?

HAROON: No, I'm going away to college.

YASMIN: Tonight?

HAROON: I don't believe in street fighting. I'm going to be a lawyer.

YASMIN: Cheerio then. (*To* AMINA.) See you later.

HAROON: Yasmin, do you respect me?

YASMIN: What?

HAROON: I just want to know if you can respect other people's minds.

YASMIN: Our people are out there boiling with rage. Ridiculous boys like you with petrol bombs. What'll happen tonight will be terrible. And you ask me for compliments.

(*She goes.*)

HAROON: Amina, there's no reason why we shouldn't be friends, now.

SUSAN: (*Off*) Amina!

HAROON: Jesus, it's that creeping journalist. You don't see someone for two months and then they're everywhere. She was asking me about you this morning in the High Street.

AMINA: I wish I hadn't missed her programme. Does she still see Anwar?

HAROON: Susan? No, she was just using him. He was just using her. I made notes. But it was over ages ago. People don't like being used.

SUSAN: (*Coming in. She and* AMINA *embrace*) Amina.

AMINA: Susan.

SUSAN: It's good to see you.

AMINA: And you.

SUSAN: (*Touching her hair*) When did you have this done?

AMINA: At London Airport. It was all over the hairdresser's floor. They said they didn't like to chop it. The floor's the best place for it, I said.

SUSAN: I just called at your house. Someone pulled aside the curtain but didn't open the door.

AMINA: They've sent a geriatric relative from Bradford to look after me. That was the only way my mother would let me stay in England on my own.

SUSAN: I see. I heard about the meeting and came straight here. (*To* HAROON.) Are you coming down to the High Street?

HAROON: No I've got to go.

SUSAN: Where Haroon?

HAROON: On a long march through the institutions. The black mole under the lawns and asphalt of England.

SUSAN: What?

HAROON: (*To* AMINA) I'll be upstairs in the other office. I'm leaving in an hour.

(*He goes, taking his suitcase.*)

AMINA: Sorry I missed your programme. What effect did it have?

SUSAN: Effect? The producer said it was utterly seamless. I want to do something on this organization.

AMINA: We'll be in action today, I s'pose.

SUSAN: I'm bloody scared and I don't care who fucking knows it.

AMINA: I am too.

SUSAN: I usually park round the corner. Today the street was full of police horses. It's like Kempton Park.

AMINA: People are calm. I went for a walk this afternoon. No one's leaving the area. They're just barricading their shops. Tomorrow morning they'll be open again. It's only the kids who think it's a bundle.

SUSAN: Yes. Amina, I know there's no time now, but I bought you some tape to hear.

AMINA: Tape? I don't think people are interested in that round here.

159

SUSAN: Your father spoke to me when he was ill, just before he died. I didn't use it. But I thought you might like to hear it.

AMINA: My old man's still talking is he? What's he say?

SUSAN: He said he was worried that you might become bitter.

AMINA: He said that?

SUSAN: And he thought you'd be better off in Pakistan. There isn't a place for you here.

AMINA: What other good advice has he left me? No. I'll listen to it later. (*Pause.*) It seems so long since he died. And you expect those moments to be bigger don't you? I was watching the telly. I heard this noise like an Indian record speeded up. I went into the hall. My mother had come back from the hospital. I said, 'It's no good crying.' For the first time in years I said the name of Mohammed, again and again. I'm over it now.

SUSAN: Are you?

AMINA: Nearly.

SUSAN: Do you miss him?

AMINA: There isn't a day when I don't think of him. (*Pause.*) Susan, I'll come and join you later on, OK?

SUSAN: All right. Are the others around?

AMINA: They've taken some stuff down to the first-aid house.

SUSAN: I'll stick with you lot tonight I think.

AMINA: Right. If you don't come back here, wait for me by the park entrance. Do you know where it is?

SUSAN: By Osterley Park Road.

AMINA: Right. Don't move till I get there.

SUSAN: Can I leave this in case it gets smashed up?

AMINA: Sure.

(SUSAN *puts the tape recorder on the table.*)

Can I have the tape?

SUSAN: Are you sure it won't be painful?

AMINA: I'm certain it will be.

(*She gives the tape to* AMINA. SUSAN *goes.* AMINA *puts the tape in the machine. She turns it on. We hear* SUSAN's *voice: 'Mr Ali, do you want to say anything else?'* AMINA *turns off the tape immediately. Pause. She bangs on the table.*)

Haroon! Haroon! Haroon!

HAROON: (*Rushing in*) What is it?

AMINA: Come here.

HAROON: She upset you?

AMINA: No.

HAROON: She has. I can see she has. I'll clout her.

AMINA: No. Haroon. Haroon. I want to fuck.

HAROON: What? Now?

AMINA: Yes.

HAROON: It's terrible, a good Pakistani girl talking like this. No wonder you freak people. Amina you'd better lie down.

AMINA: Yes with you on me.

HAROON: You want to be comforted?

AMINA: I thought I did. Now I'm going for the other thing.

HAROON: You want my body to give you sexual ecstasy like in the old days. (*He's undoing his shirt.*)

AMINA: Like then, yes.

HAROON: I don't mind.

AMINA: Good.

HAROON: You're not just using me? (*Pause.*) I didn't think so.

AMINA: You know what my father said before he died?

HAROON: What?

AMINA: That I shouldn't get bitter.

HAROON: That's understandable and everything.

AMINA: I'm not like that, am I?

HAROON: You? No.

AMINA: You are, if anyone is.

HAROON: Amina it feels a bit windy in here, half-nude.

AMINA: I want you.

HAROON: Right you are.

AMINA: Feel myself alive again. It's as if I've been buried for so long. I don't want to feel evil.

HAROON: Amina don't worry about my train.

AMINA: Put a chair against the door.

(RAVI *enters*.)

RAVI: Amina will you write a letter for me? This'll be my last night in England if I'm killed tonight. (*Pause.*) Sorry.

161

AMINA: It's all right Ravi. We've finished.

HAROON: Have we?

RAVI: Hallo Haroon. Still not talking?

HAROON: (*Dressing. To* RAVI) I got out that trouble with the police by the skin of my balls. I'll never forget it.

RAVI: It's I who will never forget it Haroon. If you hadn't impersonated me I'd have been deported. I'd be back home, washing down the bullocks, milking the cows and shitting in the fields. Instead I'm here, shitting in my pants. Thank you. Brother, let's shake. (*He offers* HAROON *his hand.*)

HAROON: Ravi, if I shake you, it'll be by the throat. OK? (*To* AMINA.) I'm leaving. I've got a long way to go.
(*He goes.*)

RAVI: That taught him a lesson. What are you stapling?

AMINA: Leaflets telling people what to do if they're arrested.

RAVI: I could give out leaflets.
(YASMIN *enters.*)
I don't think I've got the body for fighting. Amina, I couldn't come and live in your house for a few days could I? I left my hostel.

AMINA: When?

RAVI: At three o'clock this morning.

AMINA: I'll see.

RAVI: You haven't got any money have you?

AMINA: You know I've left the supermarket.

RAVI: I didn't say I wanted to borrow money. I'm checking you're OK. Are you OK? (*He moves across to* YASMIN.)

YASMIN: (*To* AMINA) Is Anwar back yet?

AMINA: No, he's still out there organizing.

YASMIN: Right.

RAVI: (*To* YASMIN) Yasmin, am I the only person in England who doesn't have sex all the time? Or are there others? (*Pause.*) Yasmin I feel so lost in this country. I can't get a grip. I'll never succeed.

YASMIN: What d'you mean? Anwar got you a job didn't he? And Haroon wrote to your parents saying you'd become a managing director.

RAVI: Yasmin, I'm not joking this time, somehow I've got into deep fucking trouble.

YASMIN: What's happened?

RAVI: I've got nowhere to live. And they kicked me out of my job in the biscuit factory.

YASMIN: Why?

RAVI: It was destiny I think. (*He takes out a packet of biscuits and gives it to her.*) Exactly. You don't want to go to the pictures tomorrow do you?

YASMIN: If the cinema's still there, we'll go. If not, we'll stay in.

RAVI: Do you mean it?

YASMIN: Why not?

RAVI: Really?

YASMIN: I've said so.

RAVI: I know, I know. Yasmin, I knew you were radical. I didn't realize you were kind as well.

AMINA: Maybe Ravi could help with leaflets or something.

YASMIN: Yes, why not. Are there enough?

AMINA: There's piles of them in the upstairs office.

YASMIN: You've done a good job.

AMINA: I'll see they're distributed properly.

YASMIN: Yes, they'll be needed. How do you feel Amina?
    (*Enter* ANWAR *and* SUSAN.)

ANWAR: It's completely boarded up out there. And people are gathering.

YASMIN: Already?

ANWAR: By tonight there'll be a huge crowd. Everyone'll be out.

YASMIN: What kind of mood are people in?

ANWAR: Not good, I'm afraid.

AMINA: Why?

ANWAR: They expected the meeting to be stopped.

YASMIN: I did.

ANWAR: Yes, it's angered a lot of us. It shouldn't be allowed. Everyone's in favour of free speech. But no one wants it rammed down their throat. (*Pause.*) Some of our lot are filtering out into the side streets. They're going to sit down in the road. They say if that doesn't prevent them getting through they'll turn over cars.

163

YASMIN: Have you got people keeping an eye on those mad kids?

ANWAR: Yes. And the Asian Workers have got their people out spreading ineffectiveness.

YASMIN: I'm sure.

ANWAR: Have you been speaking to people?

YASMIN: Yes. They're getting worried.

ANWAR: Sure. No one likes it. I don't want a policeman's boot in the side of my head. But we can't sit on our arses while those scum insult us. (*He takes out some vicious looking weapons.*) We've got to defend ourselves. Isn't that true Yasmin?

YASMIN: It's crucial we defend ourselves. But some of our people imagine that all our work can be done with broken bottles and knives.

ANWAR: Tonight that's the only possible response.

YASMIN: Yes, but I'm already thinking about tomorrow.

ANWAR: Good.

(AMINA *hands leaflets to* RAVI.)

AMINA: You take these.

YASMIN: (*To* RAVI) Nothing's going to happen to you, don't worry.

(*They go into the upstairs office.*)

ANWAR: (*To* SUSAN) I'm just waiting here for Yasmin and the others. You should be out there, soaking up the local colour.

SUSAN: Anwar, you are the local colour.

ANWAR: Susan, I'm feeling pretty jumpy at the moment.

SUSAN: I've got some good news. I've spoken to that TV producer about the Youth Movement. He's interested in a film.

ANWAR: We're very photogenic, some of us.

SUSAN: I'd like you to help me make it.

ANWAR: Why me?

SUSAN: What's the matter? I thought we had an understanding?

ANWAR: That wasn't an understanding. It was a pleasant collision.

SUSAN: Other people in the organization aren't against the idea of a film.

ANWAR: You've spoken to them behind my back?

SUSAN: They can speak for themselves can't they?

ANWAR: They do, constantly.

SUSAN: They told me their ideas are important. They want them to be heard. They are persuasive arguments. They should be used politically.

ANWAR: I'm tired of your political patter. It bores me now.

SUSAN: Anwar you're so arrogant. Even within your own organization.

ANWAR: Why don't you go down the first-aid centre?
(*Enter* RAVI.)
They'll need help there later on. You know how to tie a bandage, don't you?

RAVI: I could do that. I've done it before.

ANWAR: No. You make sure people get those leaflets.

AMINA: Everyone's ready Anwar.

ANWAR: Let's get out there then.

YASMIN: Where will you be?

ANWAR: Down by the Broadway. I'll talk to the people there.

YASMIN: Try and calm them.

ANWAR: Have you told the group leaders what they're supposed to be doing?

YASMIN: I talked to them this afternoon.

ANWAR: Right. Let's go over it quickly. We'll join up with the other group by the High Street. Then we'll march towards the hall. We'll surround it. When they're in and they've started their meeting we'll attack. If we can't get near – which is likely – we'll wait till they come out. We'll reorganize and get them as they try to get to their coaches.

YASMIN: Right. I'll try and make sure the group leaders stick to that.

ANWAR: Good. Well, good luck brothers and sisters. Come on Ravi. You're our first line of defence. (*Pause. He looks at* AMINA, *referring to the petrol.*) Amina.

AMINA: Right.
(*He goes.*)

RAVI: (*To* YASMIN) How often does this kind of thing happen in England?

YASMIN: More and more.

RAVI: Well try and keep away from the fighting if you can.
(*He goes, followed by* SUSAN.)

YASMIN: (*To* AMINA) What are you doing Amina?

AMINA: I'm just coming.

(AMINA *goes upstairs.* YASMIN *waits, then leaves.* AMINA *re-enters. She's got the petrol, and she's carrying her coat. She puts the petrol on the table, puts her coat on, picks up the tape, looks at it. She hesitates, then puts it in the machine.*)

AMJAD: (*On tape*) Susan, we were talking about the law, British law, basic justice. I meant that the law here genuinely tries to protect men from grievous abuse. But . . . I can remember what it was like before. And the day Churchill died, that winter, the English neighbours in Ealing came to us. We watched his funeral. You see he was our man too. You trusted things here though they fell down sometimes. Two weeks ago I went to the police about my court case. See this bruise here? Let me say . . . there are a few bad Englishmen. Some who are uncompassionate. But most are good. Most have treated me respectfully. The law, when it is upheld, is good here. I'd like my daughter Amina to go back with her husband to Pakistan, though. She has become English. It's not her fault. But I am afraid she will become confused. I am afraid that eventually she will become bitter, yes.

(YASMIN *enters. Stops. Watches* AMINA.)

And I don't think she will live in the way I want her to. That's not possible here now. She'll be pressured in a bad direction.

YASMIN: Amina.

AMJAD: I think she must return home and stay with her relatives.

(AMINA *stops the tape.*)

YASMIN: What are you doing?

AMINA: It's a tape that Susan left.

YASMIN: It was your father's voice. Still reproaching you.

AMINA: Yes.

YASMIN: Stupid to play that now. We have work to do. And you should be making your own life.

AMINA: I want to. I must.

YASMIN: Why listen to that then? They're empty men, those kind of fathers. If you prick them with a pin they'll explode like balloons.

AMINA: No I don't believe that.

YASMIN: Why not? If your father had lived, you'd be washing Farouk's flowery shirts by now.

AMINA: At one time, in the old house, my father had loads of English friends. They really liked him. They'd bet on horses and watch TV in the afternoon.

YASMIN: So?

AMINA: We hardly know any English people. And my father said some good things which I want to understand.

YASMIN: Tell me one good thing he said.

AMINA: About the law. He says: in India a policeman won't move before you bribe him – unless it's to hit you.

YASMIN: I'm not against things here. I want them to be improved. And for women like us, too much is dictated by other people. By our parents. And tonight by white racists. They have their meeting and we run about like football supporters. Even Ravi's found a cowardly courage in the mob.

AMINA: How?

YASMIN: He said to me, 'Yasmin, I'm determined to hit one of those bastards today.'

(*They laugh.* AMINA *picks up the petrol.*)

What's that?

AMINA: Petrol.

YASMIN: You have a car now?

AMINA: Anwar says we must burn down the hall where they're having their meeting.

YASMIN: That would certainly have an effect on their bodies. I'm losing my nerve. Put it back.

AMINA: No Yasmin.

YASMIN: Do what I say.

AMINA: Why?

YASMIN: I am afraid we might relish it too much.

AMINA: We're afraid to leave the area. People want revenge for all that.

YASMIN: Retaliation is a necessity – sometimes. But some of us think it's a luxury. Put that back.

(AMINA *puts it under the table.*)

167

There will be trouble tonight. Why add to it? It's us who have to sweep up in the morning. We can't go home like your mother.

AMINA: I had a letter from her. She says she'll never come back. Except to take me back to Pakistan with her.

YASMIN: Which you won't allow?

AMINA: Never. But she's happy now. It's such a relief.

YASMIN: She belongs there. Come on. We must make our protest.

AMINA: We'll stick together shall we?

YASMIN: I think we should.

AMINA: Shall I turn off the lights?

YASMIN: No leave them on. So people know we're here.

(*Blackout.*)

BIRDS OF PASSAGE

Characters

DAVID	Dad, aged fifty-seven
AUDREY	Mum, fifty-five
STELLA	their daughter, twenty-eight
PAUL	their son, twenty-three
EVA	Audrey's sister, fifty
TED	her husband, fifty
ASIF	the lodger, twenty-nine

Birds of Passage was first performed at Hampstead Theatre, London, on 15th September 1983. The cast was as follows:

STELLA	Belinda Sinclair
PAUL	Neil Pearson
DAVID	Joe Melia
AUDREY	Jean Boht
EVA	Rowena Cooper
ASIF	Raad Rawi
TED	Roger Sloman
Director	Howard Davies
Designer	Sue Plummer

Act One

SCENE ONE

PAUL *is playing the piano upstairs.* STELLA *comes on, carrying a suitcase.*

STELLA: (*Calling*) Mum. (*Pause.*) Mum. Dad.
    (PAUL *begins to sing as he plays.*)
    Paul, can you stop that?
    (*He continues.*)
    Look what I've brought you.
    (*He stops. Pause. He continues.*)
    Duty-free.
    (*He stops. He appears.*)

PAUL: (*Singing at her*) 'I ain't good-looking babe, and I don't dress fine –'

STELLA: Aren't they here? I rang to say I was coming.

PAUL: And they went out. (*Singing*) 'But I'm a travelling woman with a travelling mind.' You've come all this way. Chelsea, isn't it?

STELLA: I've been in Paris for two months.

PAUL: What's it like? I've never even been on a plane.
    (*She indicates to him and he goes to her. He hugs her.*)
    Love your clothes, your smell, everything. Kiss you.
    (*But he licks her.*)

STELLA: Bloody fool. (*She produces a bottle of whisky from her bag.*)

PAUL: Here. You obviously love your brother. (*He bangs a nearby chair enthusiastically.*) Relax. They've only gone up Sydenham Station in Auntie Eva's car.

STELLA: It's so long since I've been here.

PAUL: Eight months.

STELLA: Do they resent that? Oh, why should they? Sydenham's a leaving place.

PAUL: Oh yes.

STELLA: You'll get out of South London, won't you, Paul?

PAUL: 'Course, but where is there?

173

STELLA: When I was a kid and had 'flu I lay on the sofa and
      looked at the wallpaper for hours. It'll still be marked where
      I scribbled on it. Sorry I haven't had time to ask you up for
      lunch.

PAUL: How is being in South London like being hit with a fish?

STELLA: I don't know. How is it like being hit with a fish?

PAUL: It keeps you awake, in a funny kind of way. Those lunches
      are a high point with me. Clever people dropping in. Been
      busy at the language school, I expect. I have seen you, Stella.
      (*He gives her the bottle. She drinks.*)
      I've watched you.
      (*She hands back the bottle. He looks at it.*)
      Lipstick.

STELLA: Have you been following me?

PAUL: How did you get it inside the rim? (*He licks round the rim.*)
      When I saw you, Stel, you were drinking a drink with
      cucumbers in. This was at the Mozambique Club. You
      remember? I would have asked you for money.

STELLA: You unemployed?

PAUL: 'Course. But if I could get work I'd run ten miles. I want
      more than a job.

STELLA: D'you know what you want?

PAUL: You left the ol' Mozambique with a foreigner who had on a
      green suit and sweat on his head. You walked right past me.
      I could have put my hand up your skirt.

STELLA: You didn't.

PAUL: You didn't seem anything to do with me. You could have
      been anyone. I have envied you. And there you were in the
      Mozambique, having a hectic time in leopardskin trousers,
      with a face as human as a potato. Who was the old man?

STELLA: How did you get into the Mozambique?

PAUL: Toilet window. You too?

STELLA: You appear in those places now?

PAUL: 'Bout once a week I have a bit of fun up London. Rest of
      the time I'm roaming round here.

STELLA: Who's behind this?

PAUL: A friend of mine. Asif. He specializes in leading people
      into trouble.

174

STELLA: (*Picking up her bag*) I'll put this upstairs.

PAUL: Are you intending to sleep in the same bed as the new lodger they've just gone to pick up? He's got your room. He's attractive, but it's early days.

STELLA: Who is he?

PAUL: He's a quiet student, at Imperial College. Mum told you she's being laid off, didn't she?

STELLA: I love her more than anyone.

PAUL: Late.

STELLA: I thought about her every day in France.

PAUL: She bores us all to bleedin' death.

STELLA: What's the lodger's name?

(*Noise outside.*)

DAVID: (*Off*) Get round, Audrey, and open that door. I'll twist this round, twist this round and hold it up. (*He strains.*) Yes! Now!

EVA: (*Off*) You're on the front of my shoe, David, and you didn't say we'd be moving furniture!

DAVID: (*Off*) Out the way you useless woman!

STELLA: Who is he?

(PAUL *snatches the bottle from her and swigs.*)

You bloody little animal.

AUDREY: (*Off*) I'm not doing any more.

DAVID: (*Off*) Oh yes you are.

PAUL: Don't look scared. We're family.

STELLA: Auntie Eva with them?

PAUL: Yeah.

ASIF: (*Off*) Mr Bareham.

DAVID: (*Off*) Asif, what? What?

ASIF: (*Off*) I think the paint's coming off the wall just here.

DAVID: (*Off*) The fucking house is round our ankles. (*Shouting.*) Paul! Are you in there, Paul?

PAUL: (*Shouting*) I'm in here, yes.

DAVID: (*Off, shouting*) If you're in there, then get out here, you bloody fool!

(PAUL *goes out.* STELLA *prepares herself. Then they all enter, carrying Asif's trunk.* EVA *is well-dressed.* AUDREY *sees* STELLA.)

AUDREY: My baby's here. (*She lets go of her bit of the trunk*.)

PAUL: (*Taking the weight*) Jesus, Mum.

    (*They put the trunk down.* AUDREY *embraces* STELLA. ASIF *and* PAUL *shake hands*.)

STELLA: (*To* AUDREY) Mum, when did you get glasses?

AUDREY: Hasn't she got a nice coat on?

EVA: (*Fingering the coat*) Hallo, my love. Tough leather's back in is it?

STELLA: Auntie Eva.

PAUL: (*To* ASIF) You got here, eh?

EVA: (*To* AUDREY) Remind me to give you my skunk-skin hat.

PAUL: (*To* ASIF) You're miles from everything, you know that?

AUDREY: There's a shopping centre. A canal, and –

DAVID: He wants to study, not rumba.

    (ASIF *nods*.)

    I know the feeling.

AUDREY: (*Indicating* STELLA) My only daughter, Stella.

STELLA: Hallo.

EVA: (*Looking at the label on the trunk*) Defence Housing, Karachi. Pakistan. You're Pakistani.

AUDREY: Let's push this out of the way. Paul.

    (AUDREY *and* PAUL *push the trunk out of the way*.)

EVA: (*To* ASIF) What a long way to have come. You're the first Pakistani I've met. We hear a lot about them.

AUDREY: Quite a lot.

EVA: I could have carried that trunk to Brazil. I wonder why I feel so exhilarated today?

DAVID: To be over here and out of your own house. Ted getting you down more than usual?

EVA: No. Yes. Yes.

DAVID: In this society we hate change. We make no provision for it. We see it negatively, as disruption.

ASIF: (*Interested*) Why?

DAVID: We cling on to things. (*To* EVA.) Leave him.

EVA: I'm fond of our garden. You haven't seen the rock garden.

DAVID: I'm not moved by rocks.

EVA: You never come over now, neither of you.

DAVID: You're welcome here. If it makes life easier, Eva.

176

EVA: It's a long time since you've been so nice to me.

DAVID: I don't mean to be.

PAUL: (*To* ASIF, *brandishing a coin*) Heads or tails! A quid! Heads?

AUDREY: (*To* ASIF) Are you feeling peckish, duck?

ASIF: Sorry?

EVA: He's ravishing, I bet –

(PAUL *tosses the coin and holds it covered on the back of his hand*.)

PAUL: (*Uncovering it*) You've won son. As always.

EVA: (*To* ASIF) I'll get him a nice corned-beef sandwich.

(EVA *exits*.)

DAVID: (*To* STELLA) Painful to be home?

STELLA: Why should I rush here? You usually only want me to vote at one of your meetings.

AUDREY: (*To* ASIF) Sit down.

DAVID: (*To* ASIF) Make yourself comfortable.

AUDREY: (*To* ASIF) David made us all join his Labour Party. So when he wants to pass a motion we all have to go and vote. I usually drop off because I do physical work in my job. But he bangs me and says: vote you stupid woman! Get yer hand up!

PAUL: I went past Clem Attlee House this morning.

DAVID: Oh yeah?

PAUL: (*To* ASIF) That's the Party headquarters. (*To* DAVID.) There wasn't a pane of glass left in it. Is that to make the party more accessible?

STELLA: (*To* DAVID) How can you sit through those endless meetings with those mediocre bores going on?

DAVID: I've sometimes thought it my duty to see that things get done, in housing or education and so on. I thought big organizations could make small improvements in people's lives.

STELLA: (*To* AUDREY) He's disillusioned.

DAVID: I know now I should have started my own commune, my own school or –

AUDREY: I hate this rotten area now. It seems warm to me, waiting for trouble. All the different kinds of people they've got here, mixed up like bad ingredients. (*To* DAVID.) You

177

can feel it can't you? This'll be the year, you said. The summer.

DAVID: – or I should have set up a house for the homeless and distressed to run themselves. I lacked confidence, confidence.

AUDREY: (*To* ASIF) Did you see that sofa? Some beast left a sofa on the pavement outside the house. I can remember when the milkman had a horse. (*To* DAVID.) Show Asif round the mansion.

DAVID: (*To* ASIF, *as they go*) A touch of damp sometimes collects at the top of the wall in your room. If it rains put your shoes under the bed.

(DAVID *and* ASIF *exit.*)

AUDREY: (*To* STELLA) I rang you and rang you.

STELLA: I stayed on in Paris.

AUDREY: Doing what, dear?

PAUL: Looking at galleries, reading, going to plays, strolling –

AUDREY: I'm leaving my job but I don't care, Stella.

PAUL: She does care. But you know what Dad said?

AUDREY: (*To* PAUL) Please turn on Asif's electric blanket.

PAUL: Dad said: You're just beginning. The elder Cato started to learn Greek at eighty.

(EVA *comes in, bearing sandwiches.*)

EVA: Corned-beef's all right for Pakis, isn't it?

PAUL: (*Leaving, to* STELLA) You kip in my bed. I'm taking the last train up London tonight. Louisa's Club has re-opened. I expect you went to the opening party. Asif did.

EVA: As long as Audrey gets her rent every week. To be honest I wouldn't be certain that . . .

STELLA: Eva you can tell, can't you? Asif smells . . . of money.

AUDREY: Oh yes.

EVA: I'd better cut the crusts off these, then.

PAUL: Don't tell Dad, but Asif's father used to make armaments. He's in ventilators now.

AUDREY: We're all right for the summer then.

PAUL: But he likes to turn the financial tap off and on, to keep ol' Asif gasping. I've known Asif so poor he had to borrow my shirt. A week later he'd fly to Venice still wearing it.

178

(*He goes.*)

AUDREY: (*To* STELLA) Stay a while, Stella.

STELLA: Till tomorrow, Mum.

EVA: Your father might be made redundant too.

AUDREY: We won't be able to keep up this house.

EVA: (*To* STELLA.) What d'you think of that?

STELLA: I haven't lived here for years.

EVA: When we were cleaning out your old room for Asif we found drugs on top of the curtain pelmet.

AUDREY: (*To* STELLA) You must have forgotten where you hid them.

EVA: She was never here, really. Out hitch-hiking.

AUDREY: You wanted new things, didn't you, love?

STELLA: I do now, all the time.

EVA: Most normal people don't run away from their mum and dad at seventeen.

STELLA: The end of the sixties, it was.

AUDREY: You went to Africa and India.

STELLA: And Russia. But none of it was to leave you. Neither of you should ever suggest it was, okay?

EVA: (*Rising*) I've started something. Bye Aud.

AUDREY: Your friends from school still live in this road. Or they've bought houses in Dartford.

STELLA: I can't think of an explanation.

(ASIF, DAVID *and* PAUL *enter.*)

DAVID: (*To* ASIF) We'll make sure you're left in peace. We respect learning.

ASIF: (*To* AUDREY) There's two whole rooms full of books up there. (*To* DAVID.) Have you read them all?

AUDREY: He used to be down here reading at five in the morning, before going to work, wearing gloves it was so cold. Now I don't let you start till six, do I?

ASIF: I bought my father a book once. It was in two volumes and it stayed on his desk for six months.

PAUL: (*To* DAVID) D'you think any of your learning's got you anywhere?

ASIF: Until one day Papa had a rage because my sister failed her law exam. He threw one volume at her and the other at a servant.

179

EVA: A servant?

ASIF: And Papa shouted, as the servant fled: let him see it! While I'm wearing out my eyes on books I'm losing money to keep this blasted rotten family going!

PAUL: (*To* DAVID) Unless they've stopped asking you to sweep up in that printers' you've given your life to.

AUDREY: He does the paperwork.

DAVID: Kafka wrote –

PAUL: (*To* AUDREY) I've seen him sweeping up.

DAVID: Kafka wrote: 'A book must be an ice-axe to smash the sea frozen inside us.'

EVA: Quiet a minute. I've got to go and I haven't heard what the servant said about the book. Asif.

ASIF: Illiterate. But with a bump now on his head. He was my favourite servant. He brought me up. But if he died they wouldn't tell me.

EVA: Why not? Why not?

DAVID: (*To* ASIF) You're a real student, at least.

AUDREY: You can't do wrong in his eyes. Our son's a bum, you see.

DAVID: I didn't read anything until I was twenty-eight. I'd already been working for thirteen years, thirteen years!

STELLA: What was it?

DAVID: The author had me in mind. 'Midway this way of life we're bound upon, I woke to find myself in a dark wood, where the right road was wholly lost and gone.' I read it in the train between Sydenham and London Bridge, the slowest journey in the world. You have to stand for an hour in fetid air with the point of an umbrella in your kidney.

EVA: You were a clerk in that tax office.

DAVID: 'Where the right road was wholly lost – '

PAUL: Crap, in my opinion. South London's a zoo. Quotes can't help you. Like everyone else round here now, I live off my wits.

DAVID: But you live off mine, off mine.

PAUL: In so many ways armies have trampled over you two. No one's going to make me redundant.

EVA: Difficult. Now go and lie down under my car.

180

STELLA: (*To* EVA) I thought Uncle Ted was going to buy you a
    new Volvo?

EVA: He would. But I hardly use the car I've got, now we've got
    the video. (*To* ASIF.) You know, Ted my husband says you
    won't find a better motor mechanic in Penge than this boy.
    He could have got somewhere. (*To* AUDREY.) Why ever did
    you let him give it up? (*To* ASIF.) Ted wasn't scared of
    starting with nothing.

DAVID: Eva.

EVA: We own a central-heating firm now with eight people under
    us.

DAVID: Isn't he laying four of them off?

AUDREY: Is he? Is he?
    (*Pause.*)

EVA: (*To* ASIF) So if you want to see what England's really like,
    come out to Chislehurst sometime.

ASIF: What is there?

DAVID: Eva's rocks.

EVA: Our big house. My lawn, my flowers, my trees. And my
    honeysuckle along the back wall.

DAVID: Chislehurst, Kent. Where Marlowe wrote 'Hero and
    Leander'.

ASIF: When was this?

DAVID: May it was. 1593. 1593.
    (EVA *and* PAUL *go.*)

AUDREY: Eva. Eva. (*To* DAVID.) It's not true that Ted's laying
    them off, is it?

DAVID: Yes, it's true.

AUDREY: Don't tell me now. (*To* ASIF.) Hot chocolate or
    something else? Milk? (*To* DAVID.) Wait a minute. I think
    I'd better know straight away.

DAVID: (*To* AUDREY) I bumped into little Dennis who works for
    Ted.

STELLA: (*To* ASIF) It's a miserable run-down area but I hope you
    get your work done. What are you studying?

ASIF: I'd like you to come out with me tonight. (*Pause.*) All right,
    I'll persuade you later. (*He goes to his trunk.*)

AUDREY: David.

DAVID: I bumped into Dennis. He's staying with the firm a bit longer. But Ted's practically bankrupt, practically bankrupt.

AUDREY: You feel slightly they've been too proud with us, don't you? But we don't want them to suffer, do we?

DAVID: They're on scuffed knees already.

AUDREY: Poor Eva. (*To* ASIF.) I'll get your hot milk and bring it to you in bed.

ASIF: Mrs Bareham. Tomorrow I must start to work.

AUDREY: Sorry, love?

ASIF: Tomorrow I may become a saint. But for tonight Paul's recommended a good club near here.

AUDREY: You're my new son, so you stay in. There's gangs that come down from the estate at night that wouldn't like you. I can't describe that estate to you.

STELLA: Isn't that because you haven't been there?

DAVID: She hasn't been to hell either.

(STELLA *kisses* AUDREY *and* DAVID *and they go*.)

STELLA: Walk up to Beckenham. There is a club. David Bowie used to take me there. (*She laughs.*)

ASIF: Suppose I'm murdered on the way by frustrated working class?

STELLA: Walk quickly.

ASIF: I think I'm going to like your family. I've been in England three years but I haven't got to know a real family yet. I intend to learn all about English life. Go right into it. And the summer's nearly here. I'll be able to study. I'll have no alternative here. Will I? I feel so happy in anticipation. I just want to laugh.

STELLA: Don't restrain yourself because of me, Asif.

ASIF: Not at anything specific. But only because I've wasted my life until now.

STELLA: Why have you encouraged Paul to waste his life?

ASIF: What?

A month later. The sound of a large motor-mower off-stage. The French windows are open on to the garden. ASIF *comes in from the garden, wearing shorts and a bright shirt. He cuts a piece of cake and goes back into garden with it.* EVA *and* AUDREY *come in. They have been gardening.*

AUDREY: Dirt on you.
    (*She bangs the dirt off Eva's skirt.*)
EVA: What would you have done with that lawn if I hadn't brought that big mower up here?
AUDREY: I think I've got St Vitus's Dance.
EVA: Your David can't have pulled out a weed for years. Nor has Paul.
AUDREY: Where has he been the last three days?
EVA: I expect he's in trouble. Asif could have helped with the long grass instead of sitting in that deckchair.
AUDREY: I wouldn't ask him. David's got a name for him: Oblomov.
    (*Incomprehension from* EVA.)
    It's a dig.
EVA: He's only been here for a month.
AUDREY: Asif's idea of a working day is a lie-in, a walk, a lie down and an evening out before bed. In between – he eats.
    (*Putting a chair out.*) I've got to talk to you.
EVA: It's a sitting down subject? Oh dear. We've had a lovely day.
AUDREY: (*Taking her hat off*) David says this hat is made of crushed canaries.
EVA: Ted bought it for me in Barcelona.
AUDREY: I only wear it for gardening. Now, you come here nearly every day now. Why? Why don't you say what's going on? Say what's gone wrong. Please
EVA: We're nearly bankrupt. We're finished. Ted says –
    (ASIF *comes in from the garden. He goes to the far side of the room and sits.*)
AUDREY: How will we get that mower back to your car?
EVA: Leave it.
AUDREY: That monster.

EVA: Ted says he's going to sell my car. The recession's broken us in two. It's true. You could tell. Don't pretend.

AUDREY: Let's go into the kitchen.

EVA: He's stopped giving me money. To get me used to the situation. To help me appreciate the seriousness of our decline. And I haven't got money of my own. How will I buy food to avoid starvation? I said to him.

AUDREY: Yes.

EVA: You lose a few pounds sterling and then a few pounds weight, he said, then I'll reconsider.

AUDREY: Bloody beast he is.

EVA: I sold the blender to the little woman who comes in to clean. Then I concentrated on his things. And some beautiful gifts people brought to our house when people came regular.

AUDREY: What's he say?

EVA: Of an evening he sits there with his accounts all over the mahogany table in the big lounge. If you tip-toe in and ask him anything, he looks at you with a face like Christ with the nails going in.

AUDREY: You built that firm together. He's got no right.

EVA: The last five years I haven't been involved. It was successful once. It ran itself. I thought it would go on and on.

AUDREY: This morning I thought: now I'm unemployed I'll stay here in bed till David gets home. Our best days are gone.

EVA: Not mine.

AUDREY: What are you going to do? (*Pause.*) No, Eva. Not all that again.

EVA: Get the kettle on, love. (*She looks at* ASIF.) I'll have a think.

AUDREY: (*Whispering*) And not with him. No Eva.

EVA: (*Calling*) Asif!

AUDREY: No.

EVA: (*Calling*) Would you like a drink?
   (*Exit* AUDREY, EVA *goes to* ASIF.)
   You're an engineer aren't you?

ASIF: Not at this rate.

EVA: I'm not lugging that lawn-mower home. You don't know anyone who'd buy it, do you?

ASIF: I know rich people in London with lawns, yes.

184

EVA: Don't do it as a favour.

ASIF: I told you, my father spoils me. But only in spurts. So I buy and sell and take a commission.

EVA: D'you like ponds? We must drive to Keston to see some.

ASIF: You've still got the car?

EVA: For now. You can drive it if you want.

ASIF: I wanted to say . . . I enjoyed our talk on Sunday.

EVA: Didn't I drink too much? You hardly said anything. I want to know your opinion.

ASIF: On what subject?

EVA: What else is there? Our country. Perhaps you don't want to embarrass me. D'you like England?

ASIF: Of course.

EVA: Be honest.

ASIF: I've lived elsewhere, you see. Karachi, Poona, Dubai – where the workers go off at six in cattle trucks and it's too hot to stand on the balcony. Places where nothing works; places where you go into prison and never come out if you don't bribe the right person. But I'm aware that Asian people are hounded and persecuted here.

EVA: Some.

ASIF: Your husband Ted turns off the TV when a black face appears.

EVA: Has Paul said that behind my back?

ASIF: Yes.

EVA: I'll sell the television. We used to know Jews. All sorts came to the house for dinner parties. Twenty people at a time. I'd wear dresses worth a hundred pounds.

ASIF: In Karachi, when my father's feeling hot-headed, he won't sit next to whites. Yet he was a pilot in the RAF. They gave him the MBE. You mustn't look for rationality.

EVA: So he's high-up?

ASIF: In Pakistan no one can touch him. The last time he came here someone spat on him. (*Noticing her bracelet.*) It's good I think.

(EVA *takes her bracelet off.*)

EVA: Sell it. David gave it to me. I'm not old. I need money to enjoy myself.

(ASIF *puts the bracelet in his pocket.*)
My sister's the only good person I know. She's given herself to her family. But she's never been happy.
(EVA *picks up Asif's textbook and opens it about a quarter of the way through.*)
What's the specific gravity of – ?
(ASIF *snatches the book and opens it.*)
There's half a bottle of brandy in my car. I'll tell Audrey we're going out so she doesn't cook.

ASIF: It's not a good idea to tell her.

EVA: She wouldn't be able to speak.

ASIF: She'd think we were kissing.

EVA: Join me in the car.
      (PAUL *enters.*)

EVA: Where've you been, naughty boy?

PAUL: You're not my mother.

EVA: At a party, I expect. Several parties. Over several days.

PAUL: (*To* ASIF) What a houseboat that randy Maria's got. I didn't realize. You've seen it haven't you?

EVA: What did you do on it?

PAUL: We swam on it. Danced on it. We did everything on it. In two days.

EVA: (*To* ASIF) Once this boy was like my son, when Aud was out at work.

PAUL: (*To* ASIF) The girls asked where you were.

EVA: Now he's gone hard.

PAUL: Have I?

EVA: And rough. You look like death warmed up with car oil in your hair.
      (PAUL *grabs* EVA's *hand and rubs it in her hair.*)

ASIF: Paul!

EVA: I'll get a bruise there. (*She gets up to leave.*)

PAUL: (*Yelling at her*) At least I don't collect horse brasses!
      (EVA *exits.*)
      Stella says I'll have to leave this place.

ASIF: You've just got back.

PAUL: To fulfil my human potential, stupid.

ASIF: Is she doing that?

PAUL: She drove me round the East End in a borrowed silver Mercedes. Her place is chock-a-block with art objects. Round here they're fucking philistines. I'm skint, Asif. I want to get up to London again.

ASIF: Whatever you do, you won't last long with that Chelsea crowd.

PAUL: I want Maria.

ASIF: You're a baby. She likes babies. For a week.

PAUL: Look at this. (*He takes off his shirt. There are nasty marks on his back.*) Those devil-fucking bitches whipped me. What's on the menu for tonight?

ASIF: I'm afraid I'm going out now.

PAUL: You're a poncy bastard.

ASIF: What?

PAUL: Well you are lately.

ASIF: I came here not to enjoy myself.

PAUL: I thought we'd have a time. You living out here with me.

ASIF: I'm past times.

(DAVID *enters, wearing his work suit.*)

PAUL: Sister Placidus. (*He goes and sits at the table.*)

DAVID: Oblomov. Are you going out?

ASIF: I'm not Russian.

DAVID: There's nowhere to go round here.

ASIF: But you're never cheerful when you get home from work.

DAVID: I used to hurl first editions at my wife. So things are improving.

ASIF: I think you're the gentlest person I've met. When I'm with you I realize I don't know anything.

(DAVID *nods at him.*)

What are you doing this evening?

DAVID: I'm reading a book about the earth's crust, the earth's crust. And there's a woman I visit. She has a little beard, like the younger Dostoevsky. Have you read Dostoevsky?

ASIF: No.

DAVID: What have you done? I said I'd wash her hair. She may show me her breasts again, as a late Christmas present. She's fifty-one and wants to die. She's entirely neglected; I love her and practise hypnotism on her. Where are you off to?

187

ASIF: Here and there.

DAVID: Eva will drive you here and there, will she? That's why she's outside.

ASIF: She's giving me a lift.

DAVID: What kind of lift? You'd better take care of her.

ASIF: What d'you mean?

DAVID: Of course you won't. Get lost.

(*Exit* ASIF.)

Your mother hates having a stranger in the house now. Not that he's a bad boy. And we need the money more than ever, after today.

PAUL: I want a beer.

DAVID: I've had the worst and best day of my life today and your face is exhausting me. If you don't lie down I'll have to.

PAUL: If I can't enjoy myself here, I'll go back up London.

DAVID: You've become a commuter.

PAUL: Say something serious to me for once.

DAVID: You've become a commuter.

PAUL: It's dirty and poor here. It's a leaving place.

DAVID: The city tires me and the country bores me. The suburbs are ideal.

PAUL: For what?

DAVID: Catullus would have lived in the South London suburbs. They're a genuine combination of middle-class and working-class life. Bank clerks, milkmen, civil servants and labourers live side by side with flourishing hedges between them. We have comfortable houses with gardens. We are neither integrated nor alienated. Out here we live in peace, indifferent to the rest of the world. We have no sense of communal existence, but we are tolerant, not cruel. There's a kind of quiet gentle righteousness about the suburbs that I like. And there's a shallow cold smug decency about it which turns my stomach, turns my stomach. But I think the suburbs are a feature of English life that has succeeded and deserve to endure for at least a thousand years.

PAUL: Mum's scared to go out. There are gangs now. Your party didn't make headway.

DAVID: And I've lost my job. Yes.

188

PAUL: Shall I put out the flags?

DAVID: Voluntary redundancy. It's ecstasy, almost ecstasy.

PAUL: Then celebrate, for Christ's sake!

DAVID: I'll read for three hours before bed.

PAUL: How will you live?

DAVID: Without you. So cheaply.

PAUL: Yes. I want London. And a flat like Stella's.

(AUDREY *comes in.*)

DAVID: At sixteen you were thrown out of school. Audrey, I've told him, and I want to tell you that today –

AUDREY: Did you see Asif and Eva go off together?

PAUL: I'm hungry.

DAVID: She's got the tea on.

AUDREY: You know that's where she is. With him.

DAVID: We've got no income now but everything will be all right! Good redundancy money, so I've finished –

AUDREY: Why does she get everything?

DAVID: – with insignificant toil.

AUDREY: Why does she? Why? And we lose our jobs.

DAVID: When Eva wants something she just takes it.

AUDREY: We've never done that.

DAVID: That's a virtue.

AUDREY: Don't talk about virtue. We've never taken! That's why we've never had anything. But to do that now, with him . . .

DAVID: Just when we thought everything was going wrong for her?

AUDREY: Don't make me say that.

DAVID: You envy her.

AUDREY: Yes. I envy her. I envy.

DAVID: You envy the wrong things.

AUDREY: Yes, yes, the wrong things. To you they're the wrong things: clothes, holidays, pictures on the wall. But to me they would have made all the difference. What's keeping us in South London now?

DAVID: Our love of the place.

AUDREY: Make up your mind, David.

DAVID: About what?

AUDREY: About which place it is we're going to move to.

DAVID: All right.
AUDREY: Good.

SCENE THREE

A month later. AUDREY – *laying the table for a light meal: with various salads, cold meats, etc.* DAVID *is with her.*

DAVID: I think it's a good idea. A new life for us, in another place. A new house, in the countryside. On my redundancy money. (*He starts to go.*)

AUDREY: David. You aren't knocking up or anything tonight, are you?

DAVID: I've done enough for the Labour Party. We'll see how they deal with the estate this summer.

AUDREY: There's disturbances up there. So stay in. Talk to me, fat-face.

DAVID: Let fat-face get up at five to read, and write his journal and commonplace book.

AUDREY: Five years ago you had a breakdown. Whatever it was. Rest, rest.

DAVID: I'd rather not be unconscious all my life.

AUDREY: You know what's happening here, do you? Oblomov's gone out into the garden. And Eva's gone with him.

DAVID: I've got no time for all I want to think and study and do. How can they be in the garden? It's pouring with rain.

AUDREY: They've both got umbrellas. You're in charge. (*Pause.*) I'll be glad to move. Eva moved away from this area.

DAVID: To Chislehurst.

AUDREY: Up there it's another world. I need another world.

DAVID: True.

AUDREY: Don't I deserve another world?

DAVID: You've envied her too much.

AUDREY: With reason.

DAVID: No, no.

AUDREY: Her life has been a holiday. I've been a packer. We could have done better for ourselves.

DAVID: Put this house on the market.

AUDREY: You mean it?

DAVID: Let's get out.

AUDREY: Start getting those books in boxes.

    (PAUL *and* STELLA *enter*.)

    Stella.

DAVID: (*Friendly*) What do you want, my love?

AUDREY: (*To* DAVID) Don't.

    (*She kisses* STELLA.)

PAUL: I was out and about up London in the rain so I got her to drive me here.

AUDREY: We're just having our tea.

DAVID: Join us, join us.

AUDREY: Yes, I'll get more food out the fridge. Now, both of you, you mustn't mention anything to Eva.

PAUL: On what subject?

AUDREY: Any subject. Or I'll have your guts.

    (AUDREY *exits*.)

DAVID: My, Stella, I thought you'd be teaching the language of Swift and Hazlitt to lupine German industrialists.

STELLA: Yes. I've been conjugating most of this week.

PAUL: It looked as if you'd been decorating.

DAVID: (*To* PAUL) Cut us some bread.

PAUL: (*Indicating the bread*) Stel?

STELLA: Why can't we harass Auntie Eva?

DAVID: You should know their business has more or less gone down the toilet.

STELLA: Oh no.

PAUL: What's gone wrong?

    (*They share the bread,* STELLA *and* DAVID, *taking a bite each*.)

DAVID: There was a time in England, the sixties, when everyone had to have a radiator in their front room and a brand new boiler in their open-plan kitchen. In short a central heating epidemic hit the country. Ted and Eva couldn't have kids. But when did they have time to shag anyway? What with her up all hours doing the secretarial and Ted installing pipes? You'd see his van racing about the place. He'd wave but never had time to stop. People were giving him money. They bought modern cars and that mock house, 'Mango'.

PAUL: 'Limegrove'.

DAVID: Every time you visited, the walls were in a different place. Or they were extending the extension.

STELLA: And you pretended you couldn't find the toilet.

PAUL: Snob.

DAVID: Little prick, what do you know about how far they get above themselves, these people? And above you.

PAUL: They're our family.

DAVID: How they used to hurt your mother, waving that house in her face. She once begged Ted to take you on as an apprentice. He said: too lazy. They turn anti-union, these people; they talk about 'coloured' people. Finally they vote Tory, which is the worst thing, of course, the worst. And then they collapse like tents in the wind.

PAUL: They don't deserve it.

DAVID: It's happened. Because they made a mistake. They forget that in England it's always them and us. Them and us. Nothing changes that. They tried to join them. And they've been destroyed. You can't cross that river. They're in Purgatory.

STELLA: Them and us.

PAUL: (*Also imitating his father*) Purgatory.

STELLA: Those old words remind me of outside toilets. You still believe them?

DAVID: Not bitterly. But yes. I've lost interest in class. Astronomy is interesting.

STELLA: What am I?

DAVID: You?

STELLA: In this divided scheme?

PAUL: Tricky one, Dad.

STELLA: Them? Or us?

DAVID: Do you work?

STELLA: Occasionally.

DAVID: When you can't avoid it?

STELLA: Naturally.

DAVID: Doesn't that put you in a different position to ordinary people?

STELLA: In the same position, I would have thought.

DAVID: Ordinary people have to work. When they don't, they suffer. Because they take on obligations. I know you, Scorpion Stella. Feckless, independent, with contempt for ordinary people. Your smart London people don't understand the constraints of most people's lives. What they endure. So you're 'them' technically.

STELLA: Endurance. You just said endurance.

DAVID: Yes. And you will always take the easy way.

STELLA: Tell me. All the time you were reading Jack London upstairs or shouting in here about differentials with your square-shouldered Stalinist cronies, where was Mum?

DAVID: What?

STELLA: Where was she, geographically speaking?

PAUL: In the kitchen, I expect, geographically.

STELLA: Endurance.

DAVID: We love each other! We have a partnership. Why don't you bring a husband here, drifter? What do you know about profound sustained commitments to people, to people.

STELLA: What do you know about spin-dryers?

DAVID: We haven't got one.

PAUL: We have.

DAVID: Where is it?

PAUL: Mum knows.

STELLA: (*Laughing*) Parity begins at home.

DAVID: Look at her. A conversational acupuncturist. No seriousness. For her, ideas are just fashions. She's made of neon.

STELLA: Why do I make you unhappy?

DAVID: Oh . . . (*To* PAUL.) At fourteen she reacted against my puritanism. (*To* STELLA.) You were vigorous. You excited me. I took your education in hand. Sat with you every night at this table. Poured out my mind to you. And sent it out with you into the world.

STELLA: The day I left here, d'you remember, for college?

DAVID: Yes, yes.

STELLA: You gave me a book by William Morris. You wrote in it: Stella, your education is my only ambition and my only achievement.

DAVID: Ted took photographs. For an hour he respected me.

STELLA: So I went through it all. For you.

DAVID: But I wanted you to be a lecturer in a university. Or an MP. Or a barrister. What's put you out to sea?

STELLA: Don't interfere with me.

DAVID: And do you think the tax-payer educated you just to enjoy films with subtitles?

STELLA: Yes.

(TED *appears at the other end of the room. He is wearing wet, dirty overalls over his trousers and shirt.*)

TED: Just let me take off me trousers.

(PAUL *goes to help him.*)

DAVID: (*To* STELLA) I miss these talks.

STELLA: Hallo, Uncle Ted.

DAVID: And you hardly come here now.

STELLA: Families – I hate you.

TED: Looking nice, Stella.

DAVID: Sit down, Ted. Your legs must be giving way with work.

TED: How do you know?

DAVID: They always are.

(AUDREY *comes in with food.*)

AUDREY: There you are, Ted. Get tucked in. Rest your legs.

STELLA: We were just talking about you, Uncle Ted.

TED: Saying what, my dear?

AUDREY: (*Preparing him a plate of food*) That we haven't seen you for a long time. You've been so busy. You haven't had a minute.

TED: Eva's here every day, isn't she?

AUDREY: Oh yes, she comes over to us on the bus.

TED: I know how she gets here. (*Indicating the food.*) Lovely, Aud.

AUDREY: Want to wash your hands?

TED: (*Picking up some cutlery*) I'll use these.

AUDREY: (*To the others, indicating the food*) Come on, what d'you want me to do, eat it for you and then burp as well?

TED: Where's this lodger I keep hearing about?

PAUL: I think he's in the garden.

AUDREY: We aren't certain.

TED: Pour me a drink, son. Got a job yet?

PAUL: Not yet, no.

TED: (*To* DAVID) Why don't you let me find Paul a job?

STELLA: I hear you're looking for bar-work yourself, Ted.

TED: I didn't say I'd offer this boy anything myself even if he had the last pair of arms in Orpington. But I know a desperate plumber out at Dartford who's after an apprentice.

PAUL: You work all the time.

TED: I sleep a five-hour night.

STELLA: Why, Uncle Ted?

TED: Stella, why don't you pass me a fat piece of cheese?

AUDREY: I'll do it.

TED: It's a good question. When me and Eva used to come back off our holidays I used to say there must be some way of stopping this endless working.

DAVID: It's easy. You just have to vote Tory. It isn't socialism that gave you bloodshot eyes.

AUDREY: He'll have indigestion in a minute, you big arse.
(EVA *and* ASIF *appear from the garden. Both are wet.*)
Oh God. Doesn't it ever stop coming down?

DAVID: Oblomov, meet Ted.

ASIF: Who?

EVA: Ted's my husband.

TED: (*To* ASIF) All right? (*To* DAVID.) Oblomov's not a Paki name, is it?

ASIF: (*To* DAVID) I don't like it. Why the hell do you call me it?

DAVID: Didn't I leave the book on your bed?

ASIF: It's four hundred and eighty-five pages long.

TED: (*To* PAUL) What are you going to do with yourself, son?

PAUL: I want to do something.

EVA: How's your girlfriend?

AUDREY: Maria. I haven't met her. No one has.

PAUL: No one will. I'm finished with those people.

ASIF: Why?

PAUL: We've got nothing in common.
(*He goes off.* AUDREY *follows him.*)

AUDREY: Paul – don't go up London again!

TED: He's a good boy.

DAVID: Asif – eat.

ASIF: Thanks. That's better.

TED: (*To* EVA) Shame you seem to have lost interest in our garden.

DAVID: Life treating you at all nicely, Ted?

TED: Tempted to ask something, David?

DAVID: I'll chew bread, chew bread.

TED: I want to tell someone something truthful. I feel as if I've been treading water for a year. Just to keep afloat. And all the time the tide's been taking me out to sea.

DAVID: I'm sorry.

TED: I'm beginning to feel the ol' water over my head. But I'm a bit of a fighter.

DAVID: Always.

TED: I won't let my business go. Because in the end I know this country won't let me down.

DAVID: You're sure of that?

TED: What a fool you are. If tough hard-working people like me can't survive, can't lift themselves up a little bit, who can? Soon there'll only be scum on the surface. Eva, pass the bread.

(DAVID *passes the bread to him*.)

ASIF: (*To* STELLA) We've got a friend in common. The bent lawyer, Saleem. He and I used to visit casinos together. Then he'd go off with girls.

(*As* ASIF *reaches for more food*, EVA *brushes his face lightly, not conspicuously*.)

EVA: An eyelash.

TED: (*To* ASIF) You're at one of our universities?

EVA: You know he is.

DAVID: (*To* TED) Have another bottle of brown. Do you have any idea what will happen to you?

(TED *uncaps the bottle and takes a long drink*.)

EVA: I'll be interested in hearing this.

ASIF: (*To* STELLA) I remember where I've seen you before. In the Horseshoe Casino in Knightsbridge. Saleem didn't introduce us but you were with him.

STELLA: It's possible.

TED: (*To* DAVID) You walked out through Kent lately?

DAVID: No. We must do it again.

TED: I've been on a job at Edenbridge. The fields and lanes at six in the morning. Paradise. You feel like stopping work, lying down in the grass and forgetting everything. I want to preserve it as it is forever. But sacrifices have to be made.

DAVID: Ah. Sacrifices.

TED: Sometimes you have to give things up in order to get other things later on. I call it the two steps back and three forward theory, when you can't have what you can't afford. At the moment we're going back and everyone's panicking.

ASIF: (*To* STELLA) Who was this Oblomov, anyway?

EVA: Take me home, Ted.

TED: Am I ready to go?

(EVA *begins to clear the plates.*)

Eva may be suffering from exposure for all I know. But I've got a real problem. How to give four skilled men the sack. Old friends whose wives and kids I know. I believe in loyalty. I encourage it and they've never let me down, those men. Has anyone here had to sack someone?

DAVID: It's been done to me.

ASIF: (*To* STELLA) You don't see Saleem any more?

STELLA: What's the date of your exams?

TED: (*Rising, indicating the bottle*) I expect you're hiding more of this in the kitchen. So there you are, compared with what I have to do, you're all laughing.

(TED *goes out.* EVA *follows, with the plates.*)

STELLA: To answer your question. Oblomov's a landowner who won't get out of bed. A rich man destroyed by inertia. A fat vain lump of lard existing for nothing. (*To* DAVID.) We are talking about the same book, aren't we?

ASIF: That isn't what you think of me is it?

DAVID: I'm afraid my daughter has a sense of humour.

(*Exit* DAVID.)

STELLA: (*Preparing drinks*) I must go too.

ASIF: To work?

STELLA: Ted's always been an industrious turkey. It's Eva I pity. What could be worse than a woman in her situation?

ASIF: What about a woman in your situation?

STELLA: Why?

ASIF: First of all, I like you. I'm not against you. And my father has used prostitutes. I have. I don't see it morally. There's no point in Pakistanis looking at England morally – they would become insane. You have to make money, that's all. I know all those Chelsea people, the prostitutes and the gamblers. Do you work much? The way of life, the clubs, the idiots, the drinking, that would bore you.

STELLA: That's why I make a living, not a fortune.

(EVA *comes in*.)

EVA: We're off now.

STELLA: All right Eva. Sorry.

(STELLA *leaves quickly*.)

EVA: What are you saying to her?

ASIF: Will I see you tomorrow?

EVA: Yes, yes.

ASIF: They don't mind you coming here every day?

EVA: It's all right, they think I'm having a breakdown. (*Pause*.) You've been like fresh air to me.

(TED *comes in*.)

TED: I'm out at Edenbridge again tomorrow. (*To* ASIF.) Eva makes delicious sandwiches. Rub my shoulder, love. She can do a massage too. What do you think of us all so far?

ASIF: I think there's plenty of opportunity for Asians in this country.

TED: That's true. Though I would put our people first.

ASIF: I hear you have a nice house.

TED: Yes. For some reason it's . . . no, it's everything to us.

EVA: (*To* ASIF) When we bought it, I remember thinking, standing in the garden: what good days we've got ahead of us. Didn't you, Ted?

198

Act Two

ASIF *is sitting at his books. He is wearing a good suit.* EVA *comes in. She kisses him. He keeps working.*

EVA: Thank God you're here. Where've you been? Asif.

ASIF: You've got your black dress on.

EVA: Yes. The Mayor had it made for me. You like it?

(ASIF *looks at the dress.*)

ASIF: Take it off.

EVA: This isn't America, Asif. We must have something to say
first. (*Pause.*) You should tell me where you go. I can't keep
ringing here. Has your father arrived in England?

ASIF: Last night I went to the casino in Knightsbridge. My friend
Saleem lost fifteen hundred pounds, which he won back. I
lost . . . five hundred.

EVA: Which is in their bank. You bloody fool. You could get a car
for that.

ASIF: There'll be cars. All that. And I'll drive you where you
want.

EVA: Why talk like this? What's happened?

ASIF: Kiss me.

EVA: Ted locked himself in the garden shed for the whole
weekend. He spent two days down there. He wants peace of
mind, poor man. I had to leave his food outside.

ASIF: I've got news too.

EVA: What am I going to do with him . . .?

(ASIF *laughs.*)

What news have you got, funny face?

ASIF: I've been with my father. He's lying in state at the Waldorf.
And yesterday he changed everything. My suit and my whole
life.

EVA: I guessed it. He's flown in from Pakistan to take you back to
run the factory. Goodbye then.

(PAUL *enters.*)

PAUL: My dole cheque's come. Get the cards out, Asif.

EVA: In twenty-four hours Asif is going to take an exam.

PAUL: Let's get started, then.

ASIF: It's all right, Eva. I've decided that engineering doesn't excite me any more.

PAUL: What's exciting you now, Asif?

ASIF: Property.

PAUL: But you're not property, are you, Auntie Eva? (*Lying down.*) I'm excited about sleep. Stroke me, Auntie Eva.

EVA: Baby. (*She strokes his hair.*) You're tired.

ASIF: Were you at the estate last night?

PAUL: Yes. Watching for fights.

ASIF: Anything?

PAUL: Plenty. It's hot and uneasy up there. People are just roaming about, waiting for it to start again. You Asians have got vigilante groups. The racists have got their units and the police appear to be away at the moment.

ASIF: Why 'you Asians'?

PAUL: It's good to see them organizing and resisting. I thought you might feel cheered up.

ASIF: By shouting and stone throwing? Most English don't realize that the immigrants who come here are the scum of Pakistan: the sweepers, the peasants, the drivers. They've never seen toilets. They've given us all a bad reputation because they don't know how to behave. I couldn't talk to them there, except to give them orders. And I won't be solid with them here.

PAUL: Let's hope the English kick your proud brown arse right into the gutter, eh?

ASIF: There are other ways of achieving social peace. I've got some ideas. Prosperity is a great quietener, you know.
(PAUL *exits.*)

EVA: When are you going?

ASIF: I made it clear to Papa that his ventilators turn my stomach. It's a thirty-mile drive to the factory on unmade roads. When he used to come home from work he'd collapse and say: I could hire out my stomach as a milkshake machine. All his life he's done the milkshake ride twice a day. He knows I hate the filth and noise of the factory. He's decided to invest here. In property. He's desperate to get his money out of that terrible country. The Russians are on the border and those religious fanatics want to advance the country into the eighth century. Papa's so suspicious of everyone else he's giving all the money to me. It's a matter of time before I'll be able to buy something. I'm staying, Eva.

EVA: I love looking at property.

ASIF: We're looking at property now.

EVA: What?

ASIF: They've talked about selling it. I'm going to make a good offer for this house. My father said: you want to buy a bijou place that wasn't built after the war. The English haven't done anything good since 1945.

EVA: Don't be daft.

ASIF: I want it.

EVA: I know what I'm saying. All my life I've looked at houses. Our parents used to take me and Aud to Chislehurst every Sunday as a treat. We'd walk backwards and forwards past the places. You'd see the backs of velvet chairs and people having breakfast by the window. We talked about it all the time, dreamt about it, but we never thought it was possible for people like us to live there.

ASIF: Is it possible, Eva?

EVA: I'll string myself up from the banisters if we have to leave Chislehurst. Our mother worked in the Post Office and we were brought up in a grubby place like this.

ASIF: These places are sturdy as tree trunks.

EVA: In my mother's old house they'd plastered a quarter of an inch of brown varnish on the doors. We'd splinter our nails on it. What would you know about miserable houses? You had your own tennis courts. And the servants were ball boys. I've seen enough old furniture to last me a lifetime.

ASIF: Where was this wretched house?

EVA: Up by the photocopied flats on the estate. You really want this place?

ASIF: Even more than I want you. (*Pause.*) With respect . . .

EVA: With respect what?

ASIF: I think you have a husband. (*He gives her money.*) You're like a shop-girl, Eva. Get that hamster husband of yours out of his hutch at the end of the garden and screw money out of him.

EVA: You've got no understanding. Can't you see that things are coming back on us because Ted and me have had too much? It's all coming back on us!

ASIF: Don't be bloodless, Eva. Get an evening job.

(*She attacks him and they fight.* PAUL *comes in and watches.*)

EVA: Where are you going?

ASIF: I have to stroke my father's cheque-writing hand.

(ASIF *exits.*)

EVA: Look at your hair, stupid.

PAUL: Why are you crying?

EVA: Why do you sleep in the day?

PAUL: Because I'm so active during the night-time.

EVA: Wiggling in clubs.

PAUL: No, no. Up the estate. The nights there seem to go on forever. We watch, we organize, and we beat the shit out of people.

EVA: Asif's got the right idea, the brown bastard. Respectability and effort. He's not worthless like you. You were always so quick, so bright . . .

PAUL: I know him. He uses women to invigorate himself. They're a challenge. Like wind-surfing.

(DAVID *enters.*)

EVA: Why does your dad look like he's just had all his teeth out?

PAUL: He's dieting.

DAVID: It's not a diet. It's a fast. So keep out of my way, Eva. You're beginning to look like a fried steak.

EVA: I thought you'd gone vegetarian.

DAVID: It's not vanity. It's to induce extraordinary states of consciousness.

(AUDREY *enters, bringing tea and biscuits.*)

For example, in a vision I can see mum carrying tea and biscuits.

EVA: Out of the way you big berk.

DAVID: Any break in the tranquil pattern, any breach of continuity, is an enlivening thing.

202

AUDREY: (*To* PAUL) You're here, are you?

DAVID: And from now on I want to think, not talk. Not talk.

AUDREY: (*To* PAUL) I've been hearing about the estate on the radio.

DAVID: Someone will get killed up there, won't they?

PAUL: Flats have been burnt out already.

EVA: With people in them?

PAUL: The people left quickly.

AUDREY: (*To* DAVID) Pour the tea before it gets hot.

DAVID: I've had a thought!

AUDREY: I want my lie down, so hurry up.

DAVID: Tea at this time of the afternoon. Anyone for a biscuit? What an extraordinary country this is! There can't be more than two or three people who actually have jobs now. And apart from Margaret Thatcher they all work for Ted. Why do we accept it and drink tea? Look how placid and happy my Audrey is, doing nothing.

EVA: What do you know, fat-arse?

DAVID: What do you say, Audrey?

AUDREY: I expect if I sit in this house any longer with nothing to do but washing-up I'll deteriorate.

EVA: But you're going away. You talk about nothing else.

DAVID: At three in the morning she jumped out of bed and started packing a box of old clothes.

AUDREY: Yes, we're having a party. I'm going to get merry and then we're leaving London. Can't we burn those books of yours 'stead of carrying them?

EVA: They've kept him quiet over the years. We should have looked at them. We could have been cleverer, Aud.

AUDREY: Us? We might as well not have gone to school. We haven't done much with ourselves, have we?

EVA: I built up a business, didn't I?

AUDREY: So we must keep occupied now, doing whatever small things there are to be done.

EVA: Why?

AUDREY: Otherwise we'll think about dying all the time. (*She stares at* DAVID.) Looking at you now reminds me of it.

DAVID: You flatter me.

203

AUDREY: This fast. I'm getting a sandwich for you.

DAVID: No, no.

AUDREY: And I'm going to stuff it down your throat.

DAVID: Can't you let me live and let me be?

(AUDREY *goes out*.)

EVA: David. I want a word. (*To* PAUL.) Go and look at my car.

(PAUL *starts to leave, then stops*.)

PAUL: Ted sold your car, Eva.

DAVID: Go on.

(*Exit* PAUL.)

You don't have to touch me to talk.

EVA: Ted's being a bastard. He's starting to act oddly. David.

DAVID: I put fifty pounds in his hand to help start the business. July 1964 it was. For seventeen years he's flogged himself, providing employment and honest boilers. He's virtuous, virtuous in his own way. And now he's gone odd. I want to cry when I hear you say it. (*He holds* EVA.) I hear you've been selling off the rubbish you had in that house. Is there no furniture left, Eva?

EVA: There's a Persian rug I won't sell.

DAVID: It's on the wall. You'd better take a chair with you tonight.

EVA: Don't leave me, both of you.

DAVID: Got to.

EVA: No.

DAVID: Don't make a fuss.

EVA: I'm not. I'm telling you not to leave Sydenham. What will I do with myself? And him . . .

DAVID: I've no idea.

EVA: What have they got in Wales for Audrey? You can persuade her to stay. She'll soon forget the whole thing. I want you to do that. Otherwise I'll tell her about us.

DAVID: I'm too weak for this, for this.

EVA: What have I got to lose?

DAVID: It was over eight years ago.

EVA: I've excited you, David.

DAVID: Terribly, terribly at times, my fault, stupid. Weakness, before I found myself.

EVA: David, I'm warning you.

DAVID: Don't you love her?

EVA: That's why she can't go.

(AUDREY *comes in with a sandwich.*)

AUDREY: (*To* EVA) You'd better talk to that Asif tomorrow.

EVA: I can't face that journey home tonight.

AUDREY: I can't get on with Asif. I've never known a man to wear so much perfume.

EVA: People step all over your feet in those buses.

AUDREY: How d'you think I got to work all those years?

EVA: What?

AUDREY: Aeroplane? Will you tell Asif he's got to find somewhere else to live?

(EVA *goes to the door.* AUDREY *gives* DAVID *the sandwich.*)
This will give you strength for the loft.

EVA: David.

DAVID: They're not my own radishes.

EVA: Don't forget what I said.

DAVID: I thought I didn't recognize them!

SCENE TWO

Outside in the garden a party is in full swing. Sound of the front doorbell ringing. STELLA *comes in. The only light is from the garden. She puts on a sidelight. Most of the furniture and books have been packed up. She picks up a book.* PAUL *comes in with a bottle and is swigging from it.*

PAUL: You look good. (*Pause.*) Our last night in this house. You were eight when we came here.

STELLA: You won't remember the prefab we lived in before.

PAUL: Cardboard boxes on wheels.

STELLA: Dad kissed the floor when we got here. He got up and said 'mouldy'.

PAUL: I don't feel sad, Stella. I'm staying in South London.

STELLA: Do they know?

PAUL: They think I'm going to live in this house for a while. But I've got a permanent room in a place near Peckham.

STELLA: Live with me, until you find a better place in town.

PAUL: I'm not being romantic staying here. I just believe things can be bettered.

(AUDREY *comes in.*)

AUDREY: There's people at the door who think we're having a party.

PAUL: Aren't we?

AUDREY: Those roughs you know now.

PAUL: Good.

(*He goes to let them in.*)

AUDREY: Paul! No. My friends are here. The family. All the birds are in the nest.

PAUL: I'll give 'em the bum's rush then.

AUDREY: (*Following him*) Yes, but nicely, Paul.

(PAUL *goes off, followed by* AUDREY. STELLA *remains with her book.* EVA *and* ASIF *come in.*)

EVA: I've always thought of my affairs as little holidays from the world.

ASIF: That's how I look at it.

(*They see* STELLA.)

ASIF: Eva's been telling me about her parties.

STELLA: Oh yes, strawberries and champagne.

EVA: Paul and his friend Dennis would put up lights and fix speakers in the garden.

STELLA: I never spoke. I danced alone for hours and hours.

EVA: (*To* ASIF) She wore long skirts made out of Aud's bed sheets and dyed green. By nine our drive was full of Rovers and Jags.

STELLA: And bank managers and local councillors. Tories.

EVA: All the crooks, bringing me gifts. We were spoilt.

STELLA: You two lovers wait here. I want to get you something.

(*She leaves quickly.*)

EVA: We've got honeysuckle all along the back wall in Chislehurst. It actually tastes of honey if you bite it in the right place. You have to know where that is. You won't see it now. I'd have ended it myself. In time. I'd like a good cry, though.

ASIF: Please cry.

EVA: I wouldn't give you the pleasure. Here's a letter for you. Sorry, I picked it up and forgot about it.

ASIF: Exam results. You open it.

(*She does so.*)

Well?

EVA: Failed.

ASIF: Yes, but in which subjects?

EVA: In all subjects.

ASIF: Good. As expected. Don't tell anyone.

EVA: David'll want to know. Audrey says he's taken to you.

ASIF: They sneer at me, Stella and David.

EVA: From the first day David opened a book he used words to mock people who had more money than him. You're more sensible than him. And richer of course.

ASIF: But I don't have an intellectual background.

EVA: You have a white house on the beach with a squash court.

ASIF: But there, if you read a book by Bertrand Russell they think you're homosexual. One day my father was playing cards with his army friends. They snatched the book and passed it round, laughing. Then he aimed it at a lizard on the wall. I'll never go back there and be in their hands again.

EVA: Why should you? We'll give you the opportunity to do marvellous here.

(STELLA *comes in with* PAUL. *She is opening a bottle of champagne.* PAUL *is carrying the glasses.*)

STELLA: Congratulations!

ASIF: (*Screwing up the exam results*) I don't think I –

STELLA: You've bought our house.

ASIF: Yes, of course.

STELLA: Come on!

EVA: Drink to it!

ASIF: Yes, it's all mine. And I love it.

PAUL: Have you earned it?

EVA: It's his own initiative.

STELLA: (*Patting his bum and holding it*) You look happy. What are you going to do now?

ASIF: I know you're not keen on Sydenham as a place, Stella. But I can't help having plans when I walk through this area. You could buy run-down houses, rip them out, refurbish them and install small businesses.

PAUL: The housing's falling down. And the people are run-down. Will you sell them? Or refurbish them first?

ASIF: I can help other Pakistanis get established here. This area's crying out for our business sense.

PAUL: This area's crying out.

EVA: (*Noticing what* STELLA *is doing with* ASIF's *bum*) What you doing?

STELLA: I like a firm bum. But not one you'd be afraid to bite into. I'm speaking from experience.

EVA: (*To* ASIF) You're meant to be barbecueing.

ASIF: Oh yes.

(*Exit* ASIF.)

EVA: (*To* STELLA) Asif prays every day, you know.

PAUL: Bob and Maureen are here, Auntie. And Lesley. She's with that bloke whose teeth don't fit. And the central-heating superstar has arrived. In his Jesse James hat.

STELLA: Chislehurst's Mr Bovary.

PAUL: (*To* STELLA, *holding out his hand*) Stel. You and me. Dance, eh?

(TED *comes in, in his hat.*)

TED: Which of you miseries is going to dance with me?

EVA: I should have sold that hat.

(TED *pulls* EVA *up.*)

TED: Let's get it over with. (*To* PAUL.) I had a drink with your old schoolmate Dennis this evening. He left the firm today. So I'm back doing the humping myself. But can I move? Smooth like a new wardrobe on castors.

(*He sweeps* EVA *across the room and they waltz closer to, then further away from* PAUL *and* STELLA.)

PAUL: (*To* STELLA) I know where you get your money.

STELLA: What?

PAUL: (*To* TED) Go on, Uncle Ted!

(TED *wiggles.*)

(*To* STELLA.) Your living.

TED: (*Shouting to* PAUL) Four years Dennis was with us. D'you remember you wanted his job!

208

PAUL: (*To* STELLA) I found out through those people I knew in London.

STELLA: You were shocked?

PAUL: It is shocking.

TED: (*To* PAUL) So Dennis has gone on the dole! At twenty-three!

PAUL: (*To* STELLA) I bet prostitution's more insidious than you think. If you lead a worthless life you'll become worthless yourself.

STELLA: Prostitution's not meant to be a cause. Not meant to provide meaning in itself. It bought me time and intensity of experience. It paid for taxis and travel and meals. It has freed me from some tedious things. And now I'm going to New York.

PAUL: For good?

STELLA: To start a small distribution business. Books.

PAUL: Ted, you upset about Dennis?

(TED *stops dancing*.)

TED: You think I'm not human? Your friend had a great future – once! But people have got to realize they can't have things unless they can afford them.

EVA: Ted.

TED: I'm exhausted.

EVA: I sold your cameras, the light meter, the projector, the screen, everything.

TED: It's my hobby!

EVA: We can't afford it.

TED: (*To* STELLA) She must be joking!

(DAVID *comes in, followed by* ASIF. DAVID *has a large, extraordinary piece of wood with him*.)

DAVID: Everyone's carousing in here. (*To* STELLA.) He needs to cool down.

STELLA: Asif.

EVA: (*Taking hold of him first*) Luckily Ted's put me in the mood for dancing.

PAUL: What's up?

ASIF: Two stupid women were talking about me. Janet and Maureen?

TED: They're the salt of Sydenham.

DAVID: It's no guarantee against idiocy.

PAUL: What happened?

DAVID: Ol' Oblomov was behind the tree cutting buns. Janet said: Asif's not bad looking. Maureen replies: no one that colour can be good looking, however good looking they are. Asif revealed himself and there were words.

TED: What kind of words?

DAVID: Sociological ones. Asif accused them of being working class. Very funny, I thought.

EVA: (*To* ASIF) At parties you meet people you wouldn't normally trip over.

TED: There's all sorts of words I know.

EVA: 'Cept you'll save 'em.

TED: (*To* ASIF) You've got a cheeky mouth.

ASIF: (*To* PAUL) Shall I kick him out on his arse?

TED: Out where, old son?

ASIF: Out of my house.

TED: What house?

DAVID: I'm afraid you're treading on Asif's floor-boards. (*To* EVA.) Why the hell didn't you tell him, tell him?

TED: You bought this house with foreign money?

ASIF: Money's money.

TED: (*To* DAVID) And you just let him have it?

STELLA: (*To* ASIF) What will you do with it?

ASIF: It's perfect for conversion into two flats. That'll mean work and money. Because structurally the place will have to be altered. In the meantime I've got eight Indian students moving in.

EVA: Long as you keep up the garden.

ASIF: I'll turn the attic into another room, I think. And have a veranda built out there.

TED: (*To* DAVID) Where's your pride?

STELLA: Stay couth, Ted.

TED: Someone's got to say something. Our country's being nicked from us.

PAUL: By a businessman. What are you then, a rat-catcher?

TED: You're terrible, bloody cynical people. I can't believe it! You just don't care. You don't believe in yourselves. It's sickening.

ASIF: (*To* EVA) Do you want to cha-cha-cha?

TED: Don't touch him.

ASIF: What a silly man you are.

TED: No, I'm not a silly man. All my life I've given of my best. Others like me have. We don't want it taken away.

ASIF: What have you made of it? You know what the rich of Karachi say about you? I'll tell you. We say you are a Third World country. You know, under-developed. Your pound is worthless.

DAVID: Fuck the pound, we have the British Museum and the novel.

TED: He's pissing on us.

(DAVID *smashes a glass on the table*.)

DAVID: If you fight any more I'll put this into the back of my hand.

TED: People don't want it to happen.

DAVID: Into the back of my hand.

(TED *goes*.)

What's wrong with being working class? You're working class, Eva.

EVA: No, I'm not in any class now.

(ASIF *takes the piece of wood*.)

DAVID: Look at the grain of it. The shape. The colour.

ASIF: What do you think of academic achievement?

EVA: Asif.

DAVID: Not much now. Though my lack of it made me quarrelsome, resentful, perverse and obtuse for, oh about –

EVA: Twenty years at least.

ASIF: I failed my exams.

DAVID: (*Touching the wood*) It's been worn smooth by the rain. Keep it.

ASIF: Where did you find it?

DAVID: It fell off the side of your new house. You see for us education was a lit-up gate to the future.

STELLA: (*To* ASIF) I'm sorry Ted insulted you.

ASIF: We know why the English say these things.

DAVID: Nothing stops my evening walk.

STELLA: (*To* DAVID) Take me with you.

DAVID: (*Taking her arm*) Up to the Invisible Menders in the arcade.

PAUL: I'll take a picture of you two.

ASIF: I've bought a camera.

EVA: Fetch it. Paul, don't let Ted see it.

DAVID: Let's go, Stella, before your mother –

(AUDREY *comes in.*)

AUDREY: I'm having a party on me own out there, am I?

DAVID: No, Aud. Someone – go out!

AUDREY: You! Why is it always me who has to ask Lesley how the workmen left her loft?

EVA: (*To* PAUL) Go and ask Lesley how they left it. Then come and tell me.

AUDREY: (*To* PAUL *and* DAVID) Out!

(PAUL, DAVID *and* ASIF *go out to join the party.*)

I can sit down five minutes, can't I? Take off me shoes, Stel.

(STELLA *bends down and removes Audrey's shoes.*)

EVA: While you're there, love.

(STELLA *removes Eva's shoes.*)

AUDREY: Let me put my feet into those.

(STELLA *puts Eva's shoes on* AUDREY's *feet.*)

What d'you think?

EVA: I'll say goodbye to them now, shall I?

AUDREY: (*To* STELLA) Kiss her for me, Stel. I can't reach.

EVA: We'll never come to this house again.

AUDREY: (*About* STELLA) She doesn't give a bum.

STELLA: That's right. Because I always imagined there could be some other way to live. Not shut in, in these families, in these endless streets where you hardly know anyone and you become afraid of everything. And you have a deadening job. And kids, as a matter of course. Goodbye to life. So I've managed to free myself from some of the things I was expected to do.

EVA: University.

AUDREY: She wore plimsolls and left before the end.

STELLA: I haven't found a new way of living, any successful way of living with other people. Or any belief, any strong interest beyond self-interest. I haven't found my place yet. But I will find direction, I will pick up the thread.

AUDREY: I feel so happy to be going to Wales.

EVA: You won't know anyone.

AUDREY: I don't want to know anyone. There was something you wanted to talk to me about.

EVA: I wanted you to have those shoes.

AUDREY: Right. Where's David . . (*She goes.*)

STELLA: Asif's full of energy now.

EVA: Yes, but it's over. Over now. And I'm glad. He should make the most of himself without anyone to worry about.

STELLA: Can't you try to be less generous towards men, Eva?
　　　(TED *appears behind them.*)

EVA: Asif's not lazy. Now he's bought the house he'll flourish and then –

STELLA: There's someone.

EVA: Asif.

TED: Edward John Spencer. (*He shows his crushed hat to* STELLA.) Guess which wog accidentally put their hoof into that?

STELLA: (*Going*) Thank God your head wasn't in it.
　　　(*Exit* STELLA.)

TED: Home, eh?

EVA: I'm staying here tonight.

TED: We're coming back in the morning to help them anyway.

EVA: You'll be coming back, yes. I'll be waiting here for you. There's so much to do. Clothes to be packed up. They've left everything to the last minute.

TED: You don't like our home.

EVA: Its not that.

TED: You've let it go. There's dust on everything. The flowerbeds are overgrown. The garage is full of old junk. You can't do anything heavy but you could –

EVA: Oh, can't you give me just one night to myself!
　　　(*Silence.*)

TED: When have I had a night to myself?

EVA: Not counting in the shed, you mean? So what if you haven't?

TED: Pardon?

EVA: There's no reason why we should both go down.

213

TED: All right.
> (*He goes out.* EVA *stands there. Music from the garden.*)

SCENE THREE

The house has been stripped, though there might be some items they've left behind for ASIF. PAUL *and* STELLA *on stage.* STELLA *is looking at a big map of Manhattan.* PAUL *is sorting leaflets. There are some new, uncomfortable-looking chairs, which* ASIF *has bought.*

PAUL: Have they located Dad?

STELLA: No.

PAUL: It's only when you participate in a place that you feel you belong there.

STELLA: Why don't you collect your sayings for publication?
> (TED *comes in. He tries to lift a box. He is obviously in pain.*)
> Ted.
> (*He stops, half bent over.* ASIF *comes in carrying a tape-measure.* TED *glares at* ASIF *from his stooping position.*)

ASIF: I knew I'd forgotten something.
> (*Exit* ASIF. TED *straightens up.*)

TED: I won't be stopped by pain. Eva stayed here last night.

STELLA: Yes.

TED: She didn't take anything to make her sleep, did she?

PAUL: Oh no. She didn't sleep. We were all up.

TED: (*Straining*) I'm happiest when I'm working. (*He goes out with the box.*)

PAUL: Sorry, I gotta do these, Stel. Essential information. I'd want to see people got them, wouldn't I?

STELLA: (*Giving him a tenner*) Will you have this?
> (PAUL *takes it and puts it away. He kisses her.*)
> Have I got a line here, under this eye?

PAUL: (*Tenderly*) A trench, Stella, under that one. What does it matter, soon you'll be in New York.
> (ASIF *comes in with his notebook and tape-measure.*)

STELLA: I'll be staying right there for a few weeks. (*She points to the map.*) The Chelsea Hotel.

ASIF: Can you have more than one hangover at a time?

214

STELLA: Then I'll move into an apartment on the Upper East
      Side. It's got three big rooms. Friends found it for me. There
      it is. By the Whitney. That's Central Park.
ASIF: Can you have three hangovers?
PAUL: Stella will know.
ASIF: Despite dizziness, this house is the beginning of my empire.
      Hold this, someone. I think I'm going to be an expansionist.
      (*And he whips the tape out of its drum.* PAUL *ignores Asif's
      offered end of the tape-measure.* STELLA *takes it and helps him to
      measure the floor.*)
PAUL: (*Holding a leaflet in front of* STELLA) There's a public
      meeting tonight, about the estate. The police are going to
      meet the tenants. All summer it's been blood and glass, and
      now those lumpen racists are holding weekly rallies in the
      middle of the estate. It'll be an energetic meeting. Most of us
      are only going in order to walk out.
STELLA: Will you be walking out, Asif?
ASIF: All the time they're exercising I'll be building.
STELLA: You're going into construction?
ASIF: This floor could be sanded and polished, couldn't it?
PAUL: Do your student tenants know you're bringing them to live
      in the middle of a racial whirlpool?
ASIF: The whirlpool is between your ears. And we don't need
      your help. We'll protect ourselves against boots with our
      brains. We won't be on the street because we'll be in cars.
      We won't be throwing bricks because we'll be building
      houses with them. They won't abuse us in factories because
      we'll own the factories and we'll sack people.
PAUL: Will everyone own factories or only those of you with
      wealthy fathers in Western-supported Fascist countries?
      (TED *comes back in.*)
TED: (*To* PAUL) It's nearly all in.
ASIF: (*To* PAUL) You're negative. And you've got no power. You
      don't count.
TED: Get hold of the other end of this, son.
ASIF: This house lacks a garage.
TED: (*To* PAUL) Come on.
STELLA: There's no room for a garage.

ASIF: I've just measured it. You could lay a path at the side of the house and build a garage round the back.

PAUL: Where the lawn is now?

TED: I stuck those rose bushes in that earth years ago. You helped me Stel, wearing yellow Wellington boots.

STELLA: It would raise the value of the place.

(PAUL *and* TED *go off with a box,* PAUL *pushing* TED.)

ASIF: Aren't you having dinner with me tonight?

STELLA: You'll be building the future, surely?

ASIF: Not all evening. I've rented a flat near you, where I'll be living. My London friends are only interested in sex and money. I want to go to galleries and concerts. You can tell me what to read. What do you think of Chekhov?

(AUDREY *and* EVA *come in.*)

EVA: If your ankles are swollen sit down.

AUDREY: Where? (*She sits in one of the new chairs.*)

EVA: Leave some of that old furniture here and in a few months Asif'll throw it on the fire.

AUDREY: On the fire?

ASIF: But I'll have central heating.

(TED *comes back in.*)

AUDREY: Where's David?

TED: On licensed premises.

ASIF: Are you busy at the moment, Ted?

TED: I'm always busy. You always busy? I don't rely on moving furniture for a living.

STELLA: Not yet, Uncle Ted.

TED: If it came to it I'd move furniture with a will. I'd soon have a fleet of vans roaring across England. Ted's Transport. Unlike you, I can't appreciate sculpture. But I can build a cupboard in a weekend, take out your fireplace and have the strength left over to install a radiator.

ASIF: I thought I'd have central heating installed here.

TED: It's a thought and a half.

ASIF: Interested?

TED: One more box.

(TED *goes off with a box.* DAVID *comes in. He is drunk.*)

DAVID: (*To* STELLA) I've sinned.

(STELLA *hugs him.*)

I've eaten meat, taken alcohol and used hypnotism on a
political opponent.

STELLA: Why Dad?

DAVID: Not being limited by rigid principles, you see. And I've
been round giving the farewell finger to my comrades and
enemies in the Labour Party. They don't like my son.
Apparently our Paul doesn't embody the decent urges of
ordinary people. True. People like him may turn out to be
dangerous changers of things. But political and moral
radicalism is a dead duck at the polls because the electors are
vegetarian. (*He looks round.*) Everything's gone.

AUDREY: How d'you get out of these chairs?

EVA: Asif knows.

(ASIF *helps her.*)

DAVID: (*To* AUDREY) In the van, love.

(PAUL *comes in, carrying his few possessions, and the leaflets.*)

PAUL: I'm going to say goodbye and then I'm going to turn round
and walk out quickly. Goodbye.

(*He starts to walk out. Someone grabs him.*)

It's all right, I've got a room, I can dress myself and
everything.

AUDREY: You can't! Stella, take him up London with you!
Please, Stel.

STELLA: Put your one shirt in my car and get in, Paul.

AUDREY: Yes, Paul.

EVA: Go with her!

STELLA: We'll have time to talk about your future. I'd love you to
be with me.

AUDREY: There's nothing here! What a place it's become –
violent, dirty! The people are filthy dirt!

PAUL: They're not, not particularly.

AUDREY: Stop him, someone.

ASIF: He's caught an infantile disease.

PAUL: Families are divisive anyway. Why care for someone more
because they came out of the same hole as you? (*He goes.*)

DAVID: (*To* ASIF) There's a danger the water-tank will burst.

ASIF: Is it old?

DAVID: It's like rice-paper. Have a look at it.

ASIF: When?

DAVID: Right away if I were you. Right away.

(ASIF *goes*.)

EVA: (*To* AUDREY) Come on. (*To* TED.) Ted.

TED: Give us that arm.

AUDREY: I've lived here all my life.

(TED, AUDREY *and* EVA *go off*.)

DAVID: Stella.

STELLA: You look as if you're about to give advice. Try not to.

DAVID: Tell me what you're going to do with yourself. What have I made of you?

STELLA: I'm a swimmer, reader and occasional big eater.

DAVID: That's how I was.

STELLA: Will you miss Eva?

DAVID: Should I?

STELLA: I wondered.

DAVID: No, I won't.

STELLA: You haven't always been a holy man.

DAVID: By the way, what's your age?

STELLA: Twenty-eight.

DAVID: Twenty-eight. It's a superb number. The completion of a lunar rhythm you know, a lunar rhythm.

STELLA: That's advice, not science.

DAVID: Oh yes, yes.

EVA: (*Off*) They're going!

STELLA: Talk to Mum in Wales.

EVA: (*Off*) David!

DAVID: There'll be no one else, will there? (*He goes*.)

DAVID: (*Off, shouting to* STELLA) Some things have more value than other things!

(EVA *comes in*.)

EVA: Go and wave! Quickly! I feel too faint. Quickly!

(STELLA *runs off. Pause.* ASIF *comes in, filthy and with cobwebs on him from the attic*.)

ASIF: They've gone?

(EVA *nods*.)

Let me say goodbye!

(*But* EVA *takes his hand and holds him.*)

Eva! There's nothing wrong with the tank.

EVA: 'Course not.

ASIF: You know, the rooms are echoing. When you walk round
upstairs you hear nothing but yourself.

(ASIF *frees himself from her.* TED *comes in.*)

TED: They're away. David's driving. (*Silence.*) About this
heating. When d'you want to discuss it?

ASIF: Next week.

TED: Right. (*To* EVA.) Let's leave him to his palace.

EVA: Yes. Goodbye Asif.

TED: (*To* ASIF) I'll be in touch. Come over and have a drink.

ASIF: Okay.

TED: And a bite to eat. You can see the garden and Eva can do
you an Indian.

ASIF: What?

TED: Whenever she makes something spicy she says she's doing
an Indian.

EVA: (*To* TED) What's made you nice? What's made you so nice
all of a sudden?

ASIF: Business.

TED: (*Laughing*) It's not the biggest job I've had. I expect you've
got mates with property, though.

ASIF: Oh yes.

TED: (*To* EVA) There you are. That's pleased me, love. What's the
matter?

EVA: Nothing. Nothing's the matter.

(*Blackout.*)